道家養生術

By the Author

T'ai Chi Ch'uan and I Ching
I Ching Coin Prediction
I Ching Numerology
The Tao of Health and Longevity
The Tao and Chinese Culture

Taoist
Health
Exercise
Book

by Da Liu

A GD/PERIGEE BOOK

Perigee Books
are published by
The Putnam Publishing Group
200 Madison Avenue
New York, New York 10016

Library of Congress Cataloging in Publication Data

Liu, Da.
    Taoist health exercise book.   9-84

    "A GD/Perigee book."
    1. Exercise.   2. Health, Taoist.   3. Medicine,
Chinese.   I. Title.
RA781.L54   1983   613.7   82-21405
ISBN 0-399-50745-0

Front and back cover photographs by Herbert Wise
Book and cover design by Ira Haskell
First Perigee printing, 1983
Printed in the United States of America
1 2 3 4 5 6 7 8 9

CONTENTS

ACKNOWLEDGMENTS

I want to thank the following people who helped in the writing of my book: Eric M. Lehrman, Dr. Massud Farzan, James Wycoff, Mrs. Barbara Rosenthal, Aaron Wallace, Mrs. Susan Delone, Paul Smith, Earl George. I would also like to thank Rosemary Birardi, Olive Wong, Dr. William Chao, Dr. Chia Lin Song, Dr. Michael B. Schachter, Dr. Samuel Johnson, and Reggie Jackson who have helped me in the preparation of the second edition.

PREFACE

The first edition of the *Taoist Health Exercise Book*, published in 1974, has been through many printings. The publication of the second edition gives me the opportunity to thank my readers for their enthusiastic response. In recent years a number of books on the Tao have been published in the West. I myself have written two other books on this subject, *The Tao and Chinese Culture* and *The Tao of Health and Longevity*, both of which have been translated into Dutch, German, and Italian. Joseph Needham, the renowned British sinologist, has remarked that ". . . The Taoists had much to teach the world, and even though Taoism as an organized religion is dying or dead, perhaps the future belongs to their philosophy." [1] And indeed, interest in Chinese philosophy among Westerns is burgeoning.

During the ten years since this book was first published, I have been investigating the relationship between ancient Taoist health principles and modern Western science. I have discussed these principles with both Western and Chinese doctors. In addition to my research, I have continued the daily practice and teaching of Taoist exercise. As a result, in these ten years, I have not been sick, nor have I visibly aged, and I remain strong and active.

Through my research and experience I have discovered the important relationship between exercise and food intake and so present two new chapters for this edition. The first new chapter gives the nutritional and medicinal qualities of a wide variety of foods. The second chapter describes the ancient art of patting. Considered together, as they must be, the exercises may be regarded as the motion of a machine for which food and drink are the raw materials.

The study and practice of Taoist health principles concerning exercise and diet will not only prevent illness and strengthen the body, but will also lead to the achievement of a long life. The Chinese idea of longevity is not a result of fear

[1] Joseph Needham, *Science and Civilization in China*, Vol. 2 (Richmond, Surrey, England: Cambridge University Press, 1972), p. 152.

but is motivated by the desire to avoid suffering from sickness, weakness, and old age. These exercises are beneficial for people of all ages. Through practice the young may preserve their youthful strength, appearance, and energy. People of middle age whose bodies may have begun to decline can strengthen themselves and avoid sickness. And those who are old, for whom it may seem too late to do anything, may still prevent much of the sickness, weakness, and suffering which we have come to expect as an unavoidable part of aging. I hope that through practice they may all achieve good health, physical strength, happiness, and long life.

Da Liu
New York City
September 1982

INTRODUCTION

Taoism is one of the world's oldest religions, along with Judaism, Hinduism, Confucianism, and Buddhism. The origins of the philosophy of Taoism are shrouded in the mists of ancient China, but by the first millennium B.C. the basic principles were already well established. In the succeeding thousand years, these principles, with their roots imbedded in an understanding of the life forces *(ch'i)* in man, provided the foundation for an all-encompassing philosophy embracing the mind, body, and soul.

The fundamental principle of Taoism, expressed by the venerable philosopher Lao Tze in his book *Tao Te Ching (Book of Tao)* is that a fundamental harmony pervades the whole universe. The Tao ("way" or "path") is the harmonious way in which the universe functions—the path taken by all natural events. If a man wishes a long life in good health, he must follow the Tao and seek to live harmoniously with the universe.

The cultivation of flexibility and relaxation leads to this harmony and a long life. Nature has provided man with self-healing properties. Any mental, physical, or spiritual obstacles to the operation of these properties can be overcome by the cultivation of harmony. Relaxation, properly understood, is the means by which modern man may cultivate this harmony. To relax is to let go of the tensions which cause grimness and rigidity in mind and body—the obstacles to good health.

However interested a man may be in immortality, his immediate need is to assure his survival in an environment of ever-increasing competition in the economic, social, and political spheres of modern life. Maximum mental and physical fitness can be achieved only with proper maintenance of body and mind. No one doubts the need to properly maintain his automobile, his washing machine, or

11

his factory equipment. Bearing lubrication, tune-up, rust removal, tightening of loose bolts, etc., all have their counterparts in body and mind maintenance.

The Taoist health techniques are designed to release the tensions of the body and mind, and to maintain mental and physical fitness once it has been achieved. For thousands of years, these techniques have proved their value, not only in good health, but also in philosophy, learning, and the martial arts, such as the Oriental arts of boxing, wrestling, fencing, archery, and self-defense. If harmony in mind, body, and spirit is attained, not only is mental and physical performance improved, but the same principles provide guideposts for the extension of learning and the gaining of wisdom.

The Taoist system of exercise presented in this book is chiefly for physical health. It is simpler than T'ai Chi Ch'uan, meditation, yoga, and Zen. These exercises are adapted from the principles of the *I Ching,* or *Book of Changes,* and are very simple and easy to carry out.

The exercises have various names. They are called Nei-Kun, meaning good or effective inside, Ch'i-Kun, meaning beneficial breathing, Pa-Tuan-Chin, meaning eight pieces of silk, or Yi-Chin-Ching, meaning book of changing ligaments. These names have the same general meaning, differing from each other only in their points of emphasis.

The origin of these exercises is attributed to Buddhism by some, to Taoism by others, but the fact is that they developed out of Buddhist, Taoist, and Confucianist sources. To my mind, they have more Taoist spirit in their overall method and philosophy; therefore I refer to them simply as Taoist exercises.

For centuries, the Chinese have used breathing and exercise systems to prevent illness and to achieve longevity.

In the third millennium B.C., Huang-Ti, the Yellow Emperor, developed a system of curative and preventive medicine based on the use of herbs, acupuncture, and massage. The use of movement and proper breathing technique to prevent illness and to regulate the metabolism of the body was included in this system. Certain movements were used to relax stiff muscles, to loosen the joints, to aid digestion, and to increase blood circulation. Breathing techniques were developed in order that the exhalation of old air and the inhalation of new air could be achieved effectively.

Huang-Ti, who practiced these techniques himself, lived a long life, and had many wives and many children. According to legend, he became an immortal and rode to heaven on the back of a dragon. The medical techniques which he developed were kept secret during his lifetime, and were not revealed until many years later when they were codified and appeared as the first Chinese medical book, *Nei Ching*. As Henry E. Sigerist writes in his foreword to the Ilza Veith translation, "The theory expounded in the *Nei Ching Su Wen* has remained the dominating theory of Chinese indigenous medicine to the present day."[1]

According to legend, P'eng Tzu, who reportedly lived to be 800 years old, used this exercise system, called Tao Yin, and so attained his proverbial longevity. Confucius refers to P'eng Tzu in his *Analects*[2] and the Taoist philosopher Chuang Tze has said:

> When man breathes in and out, or inhales and exhales in order to release the old air and take in the new, man hibernates like a bear and stretches his neck like a bird. He is really striving for longevity. Such a man indulges in breathing exercises in order to develop his physique, wishing to live as long as P'eng Tzu.[3]

---

[1] Huang-Ti, *Nei Ching Su Wen, The Yellow Emperor's Classic of Internal Medicine,* trans. Ilza Veith (Berkeley: University of California Press, 1972), p. vi.
[2] James Legge, *The Chinese Classics* (Hong Kong: Hong Kong University Press, 1960), Vol. 1, p. 195.
[3] Chang Chung-Yuan, *Creativity and Taoism* (New York: The Julian Press, 1963), p. 130.

During the Han dynasty (206 B.C. to A.D. 220), the medical doctor Hwa T'o modeled his system of physiotherapy after the movements of the bear, the deer, the monkey, the tiger, and the bird. It has been practiced by Taoists and medical doctors in China for generation after generation.

Through the centuries in China, the philosophy of Tao and medical science have been closely related. Many exercises and health techniques were developed by medical doctors and Taoist philosophers.

Although there is very little mention of health techniques in the writings of Confucius, his disciple Mencius (who lived about a hundred years later) mentions some of the important aspects of the Taoist health techniques, such as the activation and transformation of the *ch'i,* or vital force, through proper breathing methods.

In the Sung dynasty (A.D. 960-1279), the ideas and teachings of Confucianism, Buddhism, and Taoism blended with and contributed to each other. Ch'eng Tze (fl. 1100), the most famous Confucianist of his time, said, "The path (Tao) may not be left for an instant. If it could be left, it would not be the path."[4] The meditative principles should be applied to every activity — sitting, standing, walking, and even sleeping.

The exercises were brought to China by the Buddhist master (Bodhidharma) in A.D. 530. Daruma established a Buddhist school of Zen and the martial arts in the temple of Shao-Lin in Honan province. So highly did Daruma regard these exercises for disciplining the body that they were required of all students in the school.

The Chinese translation and editing of the exercises is the work of Pan Ling Ti and is called *Yi-Chin-Ching,* or *Book of Changing Ligaments.* It is divided into twelve sections, consists of twelve movements, and teaches principles of lasting good health similar to those found in the Taoist Sutras and other writings.

⁴ Legge, p. 384.

In modern industrial societies, particularly America, conditions of life have in some ways improved a great deal since primitive times. It is true that primitive life was far simpler, but all the modern conveniences were lacking. Primitive man had only the crudest means of coping with seasonal changes of temperature; modern man has built for himself sophisticated heating and cooling systems to maintain even temperatures in his buildings the year round. Primitive man had to take his chances with regard to food, learning from painful experience which plants were poisonous. Today, information on all kinds of food, with their nutritional values and caloric contents, are provided by experts for the millions. When primitive man fell ill, he had recourse only to primitive medicine and magic; when these failed, he grew worse and died. Modern medicine provides man with elaborate systems of preventive as well as curative methods of coping with disease.

Under such favorable conditions, Western medical authorities say, it should not be unusual for a modern person to reach the age of two hundred.

Yet, as we know, the average life span today falls far short of this ideal figure, and man is beset with every kind of ailment. The reasons for this apparent paradox are quite obvious. Industrialization and attempts to "conquer nature" have brought more mischief than advantage. Today's industrialized man is, by consequence, worried, anxiety-ridden, ambitious, competitive, and dull. With more and more opportunity to "have fun," lured by the tawdry gimmicks of advertising and by the decadent delights of the modern fleshpots, he indulges in excesses of every kind—food, drink, sex, even work. Thus he burdens and dulls his mind as well as his body. This, together with the pollution and squalor of urbanized life, produces the stereotype of the average modern man: alternately fatigued and overactive, restless and lethargic, and afflicted with a variety of ailments such as high blood pressure, ulcers, diabetes, heart troubles, hemorrhoids, indigestion, alcoholism, and drug addiction.

The way to health and longevity being quite simple, it escapes the attention of those who look for complicated and faraway solutions. What goes with simplicity is order and regularity in all aspects of man's life—that is, eating, going to bed, and getting up at certain times as well as avoiding excesses and extremes.

The exercises and health techniques described in this book and in my *T'ai Chi Ch'uan and I Ching* (Harper and Row, 1972) are simple and natural, and do not require strenuous physical effort. These exercises will help regulate the blood circulation and loosen muscles and joints. With a relaxed and revitalized body, the mind gains equilibrium and lucidity just as muddy waters clear when allowed to become still. Thus, the vital energy of the body and spirit is nourished and cultivated rather than dissipated in confused activity and contradictory desires.

The harmony of body and mind is in fact the foundation and essence of all true meditation, Eastern and Western. It is not, however, meditation as a forced mental activity which is offered here, but meditation as part of the movement of life which includes the movement of body, breath, blood, and on a more subtle level, the movements of universal energy and spirit.

太極拳

如行雲流水

如道之自然

LAO TZE

Lao Tze was the pioneer of Taoism. Not too much is said about him in history books, and in China there have been numerous disputes about when he lived and wrote, in addition to many stories and legends. "Lao Tze" means Old Son or Old Baby, reflecting the belief that he was born with white hair, after being carried in his mother's womb for sixty-two years. His surname was Li, which means plum, and according to legend he was born under a plum tree—his mother was an unmarried virgin who conceived by eating fruits. Some stories say that he lived to be 160 years old, others that he lived more than 200 years; some even claim that he was an immortal from the Shang Yin dynasty.

Reliable sources, however, state that Lao Tze was born in 604 B.C., thus placing him in the time of both Confucius (b. 551 B.C.) and Buddha (b. 557 B.C.). According to many stories, Confucius visited Lao Tze and studied under him. Later, when Confucius returned to his students, he supposedly said, "Birds can fly but they can be shot with darts; animals can run but they can be caught with traps; fish can swim but they can be caught with lines. But the dragon can fly to heaven or hide underground and you cannot catch it. Lao Tze is like a dragon."

History also tells us that Lao Tze was a librarian who kept records for the Emperor Chou. When he retired he decided to go to the west of China, where he could find safety and seclusion in the high mountains; the east would soon have many civil wars. He rode alone on the back of a black cow, without disciples. At Han Ku Kwan, a fort which separated the state of Ch'in from the eastern states, there was an official in charge of customs and security whose name was Shih; it so happened that Shih was an admirer of Taoist philosophy and had studied it deeply. One day he looked eastward and saw a purple haze, which meant that a sage would be coming from the East. When

Lao Tze arrived, Shih asked him to write his philosophy; what Lao Tze then wrote we know today as the *Tao Te Ching,* the Taoist Bible. Even though there are only 5,000 characters in the *Tao Te Ching,* it has greatly influenced both China and the rest of the world; it has been translated into every language and in English alone there are perhaps a hundred versions.

Lao Tze then went to the Far West of China and never came back again. Nothing is known of what became of him, but there are stories and legends about this too. Some say he became immortal living in the mountains; some say he went to India to teach the Gautama Buddha his enlightenment. Although Buddhists do not officially recognize this story, there were many signs that he was in India and respected. (India's sacred animal, the cow, was also the animal that Lao Tze rode.) And certain Indian philosophies of nonviolence, such as that of Mahatma Gandhi, incorporate Lao Tze's notion of water: "There is nothing in this world more supple and pliant than water. Yet even the most hard and stiff cannot overcome it."

CHAPTER ONE
PHYSICAL AND MENTAL HEALTH TECHNIQUES

The core of Taoism is expressed in the relationship of good health in body and mind to flexibility and proper relaxation. An inflexible body is rigid; an inflexible mind is grim. Grimness and rigidity eventually destroy good health and shorten the life span. Recognizing these basic truths (which are fully accepted by twentieth-century mental and physical health doctrines), the Taoists concentrated on techniques to restore and rejuvenate the body, mind, and spirit. For man to achieve the goal of good health and happiness throughout a long life, his life forces must be in harmony with the cosmic forces of the universe; only when there is this harmony can man achieve a measure of immortality.

The Taoist health techniques are designed to cultivate this harmony. These techniques have proved their value for thousands of years, not only in good health, but also in philosophy and the martial arts such as Far Eastern boxing, wrestling, fencing, archery, and the art of self-defense. Harmony in mind, body, and soul is necessary not only for mental and physical performance but for the extension of learning and the gaining of wisdom.

These techniques provide a maintenance regimen for maximum mental and physical fitness. As more experience is acquired the cultivation of harmony will proceed at an ever-accelerating pace, until the point is reached where trouble is avoided before it starts.

To move through life in perfect harmony within oneself and with the universe—is this not a measure of immortality?

SLEEPING

One-third of human life is spent in sleep. Sleeping the right way is of utmost importance in enhancing the enjoyment of the waking hours, namely the remaining two-thirds of one's life.

By sleeping the right way I mean what the Taoists call sleep-as-meditation, or meditative sleep. Meditative sleep was exemplified by the fifth-century Taoist master Chen T'uan, who is said to have slept for forty (some legends say for one hundred) years. He lived as a hermit in the sacred mountains of Hua Shan in western China. Some sources attribute to him a longevity of four centuries; others refer to him as immortal.[1]

Perhaps the best expression of the beauty and significance of meditative sleep is the ballad "The Sleeping Immortal" by the Taoist Chang San Feng, who was the founder of T'ai Chi Ch'uan:

[1] Chang Chung-Yuan, *Creativity and Taoism* (New York: The Julian Press), pp. 164-5.

Sleeping on a pillow of stone
Forgetting the calendar, the seasons.
When the ch'i sinks to the abdomen
The spiritual nature will be perfect and complete.
The ch'i rises to the mysterious cavity, *
Every breath, inhaling, exhaling, natural, and easy,
Not confused, not separate;
There should be tranquillity.
One completes his spirit by waiting for the appearance
  of the ch'i
And joining it without losing it, preventing any outflow.
The real fire must be practiced within:
Up and down seven times,
Circulating nine times, with ease.
To realize the intercourse of dragon and tiger†
To reverse the yin and yang
Let the ch'i rise in the spine
Reversing the water wheel.
A drowsy man, I look lazy; I sleep all day.
But I sleep without sleeping.
I learn the real Ch'an‡
By cultivating the central fetus
When the rising hidden dragon flies to heaven. ††
This secret is learned from Confucius:
Bend your arms for a pillow;
There is real joy inside and no one knows it.
The dragon will fly from the deep abyss;
God gave this secret to Chen T'uan.‡‡

---

*   From the base of the genitals to the top of the cranium.
†   The dragon corresponds to the spirit, the tiger to the ch'i.
‡   Zen-Buddhism.
†† This describes the process of reaching Ni-Wan.
‡‡ The predecessor of Chang San Feng.

The Chinese use a variety of metaphors and similes, usually drawn from their observation of fauna and flora to describe the quality of meditative sleep. One of the famous expressions is that of Li Ch'ing Yuen, a contemporary Chinese, who lived to be more than two hundred and fifty years old. Asked about the secret of his astonishing longevity and health, Li Ch'ing Yuen attributed it to natural wisdom, including the capacity to "keep a quiet heart, sit like a tortoise, walk sprightly like a pigeon, and sleep like a dog."[2]

To "sleep like a dog" is explained by Lu K'wan Yu as "curving and reclining the body on either side, like the coiled length of a sleeping dragon or the curved body of a dog, bending one arm for a pillow while stretching the other to place a hand on the belly, and straightening one leg while bending the other."[3]

Ailments caused by incorrect or improper methods of sleep include insomnia, nocturnal emissions, nightmares, catching cold while asleep, morning fatigue, sore neck, cramps, and numbness in the legs and feet. Sleeping habits contribute to bodily and psychological pains. Habits learned from infancy often mean great loss of energy and much waking anxiety. Sleep should be:

• Comfortable, restful, renewing;
• Preserving of energy;
• Used as a part of one's meditation practice;
• An aid to achieving immortality, as in Taoist practice.

Healthful sleep is nature's method for restoring body, mind, and soul. The maximum benefits are obtained when one is fully relaxed, physically, mentally, and emotionally. *Ch'i* is cultivated by these basic techniques.

---

[2] "Quoted in Richard Lucas, *Nature's Medicine* (North Hollywood: Wilshire Book Company, 1971), p. 154.
[3] Lu K'wan Yu, *Taoist Yoga* (New York: Samuel Weiser, 1970), p. 101.

Deep Breathing to Relax the Body for Sleep or Meditation

Lie on bed (or rug) with head on a high pillow. Rub hands together to warm by generating heat in the palms. Concentrate mind on point two inches below navel. Deep breathing should be done slowly, about six to eight inhalation-exhalation cycles per minute. Rest hands on abdomen, and exhale gently as fully as possible. Keep the chest as relaxed as possible by letting the abdominal muscles and diaphragm do all the work. The arms and legs should also be relaxed. Let the eyes be gently closed. Exhale through mouth. Deflate the abdomen completely; use slight pressure from hands.

Close mouth. Use the nose to inhale gently to inflate the abdomen. Do not suck breath in too forcefully or take too much breath in. Keep mind concentrated two inches below navel, and let the abdominal muscles and diaphragm control the breathing. Let the hands rest gently on the abdomen. When the inhalation is complete, slowly begin the gentle exhalation part of the cycle, using slight hand pressure. Concentrating the mind on the abdomen concentrates *ch'i* in the central region of the body.

Proper Sleeping Postures

The hands may be used to assist sleep by circulating *ch'i* from the abdomen to the head. When sleeping on the right side, place right palm under right cheek and left palm on the thigh. Let the right (bottom) leg be outstretched but slightly bent. Rest the left (top) leg on the right leg, but more sharply bent as shown. While falling asleep, continue to concentrate mind below navel and let the breathing be as relaxed as possible, at its normal (natural) rate.

Sleeping on the left side is the reverse of right-side sleeping. Notice that the body is completely relaxed, making full contact with the bed. Arms and shoulders should be limp, and mouth gently closed. The legs must not be rigid, but must rest by their own weight. The chest, abdomen, and pelvic regions should be free from all tension. Breathe naturally, and keep the mind empty of all thoughts by concentrating in the lower abdomen.

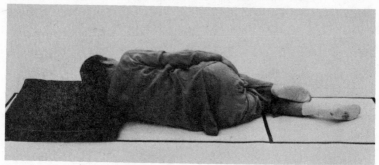

Just as no two people are exactly alike, neither are waking and sleeping habits. Even on a daily basis, the state of sleep varies, depending on the psychical and physical events preceding the sleep period. The important point is to be as physically and mentally relaxed as possible, without thought for the morrow or the past. The exact number of hours of sleep is less important. Just be relaxed.

HEAD RELAXATION

For obvious reasons, tension most quickly manifests itself in the muscles of the head, neck, and shoulders. The physical consequences of tensions must be alleviated if harm to the body is to be avoided. This is particularly important in the delicate region of the head.

Facial Muscle Relaxation

Rub hands together to generate heat. Relax jaw—do not clench teeth. With the fingertips, gently massage both sides of nose to clear the nasal passages. The moist heat

dissolves mucus, improves the circulation, and eases breathing. Massage the facial muscles near the nose in order to clear the sinuses. It is desirable to perform these motions shortly after rising to clear the nasal and sinus cavities of mucus accumulations, simultaneously relaxing the facial muscles. Skin wrinkles are also ironed away.

The area below the eyes must also be relaxed. Heat the thumb joints by rubbing against palms. Then, resting the fingers on the forehead, massage the area below the eyes with the joints of the thumb in a to-and-fro circular motion. Relax the eye muscles by frequent blinking. Never rub the eyes themselves. Use this technique in the morning, and repeat whenever tension appears in the eye region. Avoid prolonged staring; blink and shift the eyes constantly.

Heat thumb joints by rubbing against palms. Rest fingers on forehead, and rub areas on the sides of the eyes with a continuous circular motion. The massage improves the circulation and relaxes the facial and eye muscles in these regions. Because the eyes are our principal sensory organ, this area is a target for tension. Repeat whenever tension is sensed in these eye areas.

The facial muscles leading to the jaw are important. Heat hands by rubbing palms together. Then massage both sides of the face until they become warm. Use smooth, gentle, up-and-down motion. An alternative method is to heat the hands and hold them against the face without motion. The latter is especially useful whenever the skin is sensitive. This technique is beneficial to skin circulation and facial nerves.

Heat hands by palm rubbing and then press your forehead with the warmed hands. Hold for a few seconds, then move them slowly to the back of the head. Circulation in the region of the temples is improved, thereby preventing premature graying of the hair. This technique stimulates facial nerves and helps to relax the region of the temples.

Warm palms of the hands by rubbing. Then cover ears with the palms, resting the fingers on the head. Hold for a few seconds. Then gently beat the back of the head with the index fingers. Do this for about one minute—slowly and comfortably. The neck muscles leading to the head are thereby relaxed. Covering the ears is also very relaxing. Holding warmed palms over the eyes without pressure is also very soothing to the eyes. Avoid stiff neck by relieving tension in the back of the head.

These techniques should be practiced whenever tension is experienced in the region of the head. Do not be violent. Repeat as often as required during the day especially before going to sleep and after awakening. Sleep is not always tension-free for a person who is not relaxed. Try to feel the muscles relaxing and follow the movements with your mind. After doing any exercise involving raising the arms and lifting the shoulders, be sure to relax afterwards by letting the shoulders drop to the lowest natural position.

MOUTH RELAXATION

The mouth is the entrance for food into the body and the exit for communication by voice from the body. Tension in the mouth shows up in the teeth, gum, throat, membranes, sinuses, and tongue (even though it never seems to be tired). The following techniques make one consciously aware of the two-fold importance of the mouth, and also that random wagging of the tongue is better without sound accompaniment from the voice box.

First, click the teeth together gently about forty-nine times to strength the gum and root system, and to relax the jaw muscles. Second, with the lips closed, run the tongue around the outside of the teeth, between teeth and lips, about eighteen times in a circular movement. Third, with the mouth partially open, but lips closed, run the tongue around the inside of the teeth and palate about eighteen times. The tongue movements cause increased flow of saliva which is beneficial to the throat as well as the mouth.

A relaxed mouth is important for breathing, digestion, healthy teeth and gums, and a cheerful disposition. Learn to relax jaw muscles all through the day. Clenched jaws are hard on the teeth, gums, and voice box. Grimness radiates from the mouth to the muscles of the head, neck, and shoulder. Flexibility is more easily attained when these areas are kept free of tension.

TRUNK RELAXATION

The wide prevalence of backache and other back disorders, chest pains, breathing difficulties, and stomach ailments testifies to the weakening of the crucial trunk region caused by repeated bouts of tension. The following are key techniques for restoring the body to its highest state of health.

Stand in a relaxed position with feet separated. Warm hands by rubbing together if direct contact is to be made with skin; otherwise, hand-warming is not required. If hands cool rapidly, then warm and repeat. Otherwise the cool hands will absorb warmth from the interior. Gently rub the lower abdominal region with the left hand in a circular motion thirty-six times. Repeat with the right hand, covering the same territory in an oppositely directed circular motion thirty-six times This technique stimulates the circulation in the intestines and helps to relax the important abdominal muscles. Consequently, vital force *(ch'i)* is generated at the body's center of gravity. Then, repeat both the right and left-hand movements in the chest region, each thirty-six times, to stimulate the circulation in the thorax and relax the chest muscles. If time permits, the same techniques may be applied to the in-between region (the solar plexus).

Stand in a relaxed position as before. Gently rub the lower back with backs of both hands simultaneously for a total of forty-nine times. Use a slanting motion for each hand, moving them from the sides downward to meet. This technique also stimulates the circulation in the intestines, relaxes the lower back, and supplies warming energy to the kidneys. In addition, the entire lower trunk region is thereby filled with greater vitality. This technique complements the massaging techniques for the front of the body. The lower abdominal region is very important for meditation and body control.

This technique supplements the previous ones and must be done gently. Place palms of the hands against the middle abdomen and press gently. Hold them firmly while breathing softly for a period of three to five minutes. The same technique can also be applied to the upper chest region to relieve lung congestion and coughing, and to the lower abdomen to relieve pains from constipation and menstruation. This technique can be used at any time of the day or night.

In Taoist theory (as well as in Zen), the region below the navel, the lower abdomen, is call the home of *ch'i*, the center from which the vital forces radiate to all parts of the body. It is also the region containing the body's center of gravity.

RELAXED STANDING

Standing, when done properly, is an important form of exercise. In order to stand in a relaxed manner, one must use the force of gravity to provide assistance, in a friendly way, rather than fighting gravity. Then the postural muscles will obtain the benefits of gentle relaxation, which will harmonize the skeleton and the internal organs.

Gravity is the key to relaxed standing. The force of gravity acts vertically downward, following a plumb line. If the body, from the top of the head to the bottom of the soles, is visualized as dangling from a string like a puppet, the line of the body will automatically follow the force of gravity. Separate both feet a distance approximately equal to shoulder width. The soles should be parallel to each other, and the feet should point straight ahead. The knees should be relaxed, not stiffly locked. The head, neck, and

trunk should follow a straight line piercing the midpoint of the soles, excluding the heels. This applies the body weight to the broadest part of the feet. The body should be loose, the shoulders down, as relaxed as naturally possible. The hands hang beside the thighs, back forward, fingers naturally curved. Breathe naturally, and look straight ahead.

Standing is beneficial, exercising all the postural muscles and the nerves controlling the postural reflex. Internal organs get their maximum freedom during standing. Meditation can be performed during relaxed standing. Change position every three to five minutes. If the legs and the feet become tired or tense, they may be relaxed with massage.

Sit on a straight chair, or on the floor with legs out straight. Rest your left foot on the right knee. Rub the palms of the hands together to warm them. Rub the bottom of the foot firmly with the right hand. Repeat with the right foot and left hand. Rub each foot at least forty-nine times, if possible, two hundred times. Rubbing the feet makes them warm, stimulates circulation and reduces fever in the body. The feet are very important parts of the body. Taoists compare this area to the north pole. Many arteries and veins meet there, but they are thinner here than in other parts of the body. If blood circulation is poor, your feet will be cold, since this area is farthest away from the center of the body. A tale from the Sung dynasty illustrates another benefit from this exercise. A great Confucian scholar believed strongly in rubbing the feet. He proved that swelling of the eyelids could be completely relieved by rubbing the feet every day two hundred times. Taoists call this area the bubbling spring, or yung ch'uan cavity. If you do this exercise every day, it can prevent fever of the inner organs.

To soothe the knees, sit on a chair with the soles resting on the floor. Then warm the hands by rubbing the palms together. Massage both knees simultaneously by gently rubbing with a circular motion, from the inner thigh area to the outside area. The number of circular rubbings is forty-nine for both knees together.

In the event of cramps in the calf or thigh, the same massage techniques may be employed. Warm the hands by palm rubbing, and massage in an up-and-down or back-and-forth sliding motion forty-nine times.

The leg-and-foot massage technique may be repeated any time tension or fatigue in these limbs is experienced. It stimulates circulation in these areas, easing cramped or tired muscles. More attention should be paid to the soles and knees, since these are critical areas.

To meditate while standing, concentrate the mind at a point two inches below the navel. Fold tongue upward against palate (for more saliva), and breathe slowly.

WALKING

In ancient times walking was the most important means of moving from one place to another. Today, precisely because it is no longer widespread, one should consciously use walking as a highly beneficial form of exercise. Some people, particularly in America, jog for exercise, but those who do usually abandon it after a while because jogging does not fit in naturally with their ordinary living habits. In every form of exercise discussed in this book, the Taoist method does not deviate from the natural and the ordinary.

A Chinese saying compares correct walking with the movement of the wind. Walking like the wind means moving freely, peacefully, and lightly. Master Li likens it to the sprightly walking of a pigeon.

The effortlessness which these comparisons suggest is achieved by a smooth, continuous alternation of body weight on each foot. As in T'ai Chi Ch'uan movement, the body is balanced on one foot at a time. When walking, the weight and balance is concentrated on one foot—the arch—while the other is absolutely light and free. The mind is alert, yet empty and at peace; the body is straight, and, again as in T'ai Chi Ch'uan, one looks forward alertly and yet without straining. The tongue should be placed lightly against the palate. The vital breath energy *(ch'i)* is felt in the lower abdomen. All this is not only beneficial for good health but also prevents accidents.

Standing meditation follows the same principles as walking meditation, except that in standing the body is stable on the ground. A Chinese saying uses the analogy of "standing like a pine tree," which implies that one's foot should be well rooted in the ground. As in T'ai Chi Ch'uan, in which the weight is placed on one foot while the other is at rest, the standing person can alternate the weight on each foot. The important thing is that the body should be well balanced, the gravity line extending from the head to the standing foot.

Although walking is as basic as breathing, few people walk properly—that is, in a way which is both relaxed and beneficial. Walking can be an important method of rejuvenation if combined with meditation to calm the mind and spirit. As in standing, one must harmonize with the force of gravity in a friendly way. The key elements are parallel placement of each foot when it is in contact with the ground. For meditation, walking is synchronized with breathing, and the mind is concentrated in the body's center of gravity in the lower abdomen.

Gravity and body posture are the same for both standing and walking. Start from proper standing position, then shift all the weight to one leg, and smoothly step forward with the other. When the sole is in full contact with the ground, shift all the body weight to this foot. A plumb line

from the head should pass through the neck, trunk, and center of gravity to the midpoint of the ball of the foot. Then step out with the other leg, shift body weight to that leg, and so forth. The feet should be parallel and separated a comfortable distance. Feet should point straight ahead; the knees should be loose and the shoulders relaxed. Look straight ahead and breathe naturally. For meditation, concentrate mind at point two inches below navel and synchronize breathing, i.e. one or two or three walking cycles per breathing cycle. Concentrate on stability and relaxation.

SITTING

An old Chinese saying likens proper sitting to that of a bear: a kind of sitting which is at once straight, balanced, and quiet.

The sitting discussed is not sitting for meditation, but sitting in general as people do in daily life, such as on a chair at home or in the office, on a park bench, or on the seat of a bus or train. The most important factor to consider is that the spinal cord should be kept straight and at ease. To do so one should sit comfortably with the trunk erect, leaning neither to the left nor to the right, neither backward nor forward.

Keeping the spinal cord straight and free of tension is beneficial to the inner organs as well as an aid in the prevention of backache and tension of the neck and back muscles.

It should be remembered that the neck should be kept from leaning to the left or to the right, backward or forward. A straight neck facilitates the flow of the vital force (ch'i) to the brain.

Breathing should be slow and regular; shoulders should

be relaxed; the body should be evenly balanced with the feet planted on the ground. Once there is a balance in the whole body, the muscles become relaxed and joints are kept in their right position, without undue pressure or exertion in any particular direction. This is particularly important to office workers, as they usually acquire habits such as leaning the body to one side, balancing the weight on one leg, or riding one leg on the other—all of which tend to twist and distort the natural alignment of bones and joints.

Like standing and walking, relaxed sitting requires harmony with the force of gravity. This fact is easy to remember when sitting is combined with meditation practice, but easy to forget during other activities, such as working, watching television, and riding in trains, automobiles, and other vehicles, especially when the seats are deeply curved or overstuffed or otherwise disrespectful of gravity. Relaxed sitting provides maximum freedom to the internal organs and beneficial exercise for the postural muscles, provided that the head-neck-trunk vertical axis is aligned with gravity and the body weight is properly supported by the buttocks and thighs.

First, position your seat on the chair so that your lower back nearly touches the chair's back, leaving a space of an inch or so. This provides a maximum base for the body weight in terms of pressure and stability. Then, establish a plumb line through the head-neck-trunk spinal axis following the vertical force of gravity. If necessary, wriggle a little from side to side and back and forth to find the vertical direction. Do not allow the lower back to curve backward in a slouch nor to curve forward to protrude the abdomen frontward. The proper vertical position is midway between these extremes. The soles of the feet should rest squarely on the floor with the legs vertical and the thighs horizontal. If possible, keep the feet parallel, spread apart a distance equal to the width of the shoulders.

Try to maintain relaxed sitting posture during work, eating, travel, and other periods of prolonged sitting. After a while, this posture will become second nature, and you will feel uncomfortable sitting in a strained position.

Meditation during chair sitting can be done at any time of day or night. Place the hands on the thighs near the knees. The arms and hands should be relaxed. For five-minute periods, hands should be placed palms down. If the period is to be extended to twenty or thirty minutes, then the palm positions can be changed occasionally—both palms down, both palms up, one palm down and one palm up, etc.

Eyes should be half-closed, with the gaze directed naturally, and blinking should follow its natural sequence. Breathing should be natural, soft, and moderately deep. This is achieved by concentrating the mind in the lower abdomen, about two inches below the navel, in the fountain of *ch'i*. Keep the mind geographically concentrated in this region (which is also the body's center of gravity), and visualize the breath in its path from the nostrils to the abdomen during inhalation, and back again during the exhalation. Breathe through the nose only; the mouth should be gently closed. This process automatically quiets the mind and relaxes the body.

MIND RELAXATION

In order to restore and rejuvenate the body, mind, and spirit, one must cultivate the harmony of the total being within oneself and between oneself and the universe. The secret of *ch'i* cultivation is the practice of meditation, or mind relaxation. A relaxed mind is a necessary ingredient for a relaxed body. Then the spirit will become correspondingly relaxed.

The secret of successful meditation is regularity, like the watering of plants or the human intake of food. Perseverance, diligence, and quiet determination are its nutritional ingredients. If it is done daily, continuous improvement can be expected. It is not a process that can be hurried. Do not expect instant success.

For best results, two periods per day of practice are essential, once shortly after rising and once before going to bed. If only one period per day is practical, the evening meditation period is preferred. A suitable time duration is fifteen minutes; it may be longer. An absolute minimum is five minutes.

The meditation should be done in a quiet, partially darkened room, neither too hot nor too cold. The clothing should be comfortable and moderately loose. Ventilation should be adequate to provide fresh air. Noise and other distractions should be avoided.

Breath control is the key to proper meditation. Most people breathe at a rate of about sixteen cycles (inhale-exhale) per minute. In the beginning, breathe at your natural rate. As more experience is acquired, a slower, deeper breathing action is better; preferably a rate of about eight cycles per minute.

Abdominal breathing is proper breathing. A baby breathes from the abdomen, an adult from the chest, an elderly person from the throat, and a dying man from the mouth. The more the muscles of the trunk—including the chest, diaphragm, rib cage, and abdominal muscles—are used for breathing, the more the lungs are provided with fresh air and the elasticity of the body maintained or restored.

Good health, a sound mind in a sound body, and longevity are among the rewards derived from daily meditation practice keyed to abdominal breathing and mind relaxation. This emphasis on meditation practice and breath-and-mind control is a hallmark of all of the Far Eastern religions and martial arts.

Sit on a cushion about two inches high. The legs may be crossed in a tailor's position, with the ankles resting on the floor, or in a half-lotus position, with one foot up on the other. Clasp the hands, using the thumb to interlock as shown, and rest them comfortably on the legs. Let your shoulders and body relax, but not slump. A plumb line through the head-neck-trunk spinal axis should follow the vertical force of gravity. The lower back should be vertical and the upper torso should rest squarely on the lumbar region. If necessary, wriggle a little from side to side and back and forth to find the proper vertical direction.

The objective is to concentrate the mind in the *tan-t'ien* (the body's center of gravity region about two inches below the navel). Before starting the regulated breathing, click

the teeth together forty-nine times and moisten the lips with the tongue thirty-six times. Then move the tongue inside the mouth from left to right and up and down about thirty-six times to fill the mouth with saliva. Stick the tongue to the palate of the mouth gently—no excessive force is required. Keep the teeth and lips parted just a little to avoid jaw clenching and grimness. Inhale through the nostrils and exhale through the mouth three times with long, deep breaths to clear impure air from the passages and lungs. Then let your eyes half-close and let your gaze fall naturally to some point on the floor in front of you. Let eye blinking be natural.

Concentrate your mind on the lower abdomen. Inhale through the nostrils, drawing the breath down to the lower abdomen deeply, slowly, and softly, lips gently closed. Exhale gently through both nostrils and mouth together, letting the natural relaxation of the diaphragm and the abdominal muscles do the work. Aim for a breathing rate of eight inhale-exhale cycles per minute. Repeat this set of controlled breaths fifty times (this requires about six or seven minutes for an eight-cycles-per-minute rate). Repeat the set of fifty breaths if fifteen minutes are available for the meditation practice. One set of fifty breaths fixes the minimum period.

The cultivation of harmony or *ch'i* cannot, by its very nature, be purely physical or purely mental. Although the Taoist techniques are described here in terms of physical relaxation, their full benefits cannot be realized without an accompanying emotional relaxation. Physical tension is generally the external manifestation of internal tension. Even in cases where there is an obvious physical cause for the tension, there are usually reinforcing psychological stimuli. Meditation will relieve internal tension through the cultivation of inner and outer harmony of mind, body, and spirit. The results are proportional to the practice, and the benefits are cumulative. A word to the wise is sufficient.

CHAPTER TWO

THE LONGEVITY EXERCISES OF MASTER LI CH'ING YUEN

BIOGRAPHY OF MASTER LI CH'ING YUEN

Li Ch'ing Yuen was born in 1678, during the reign of K'ang Hsi of the Manchu dynasty. His birthplace was Kuei-Chou province, in the mountainous regions of southwest China. He later moved to Szechuan province.

By profession, Li Ch'ing Yuen was an herbalist. There is a story of how he came by this trade. One day, when he was a boy of eleven playing in his village, he met three traveling herbalists. They came from distant places, one from Kiang-Shi, the others from the northeast provinces. The talk of these strangers interested Li Ch'ing Yuen very much, and he decided to travel with them and learn the art of medical herbs. He and his teachers journeyed in high mountains, through Shensi, Kansu, Sinkiang, Manchuria, Tibet, Annam, and Siam. Sometimes they encountered dangerous situations, such as meeting with lions, tigers, and poisonous snakes. But Li Ch'ing Yuen learned from the skill and experience of his teachers to overcome these and other difficulties. They walked quickly, like monkeys.

LI CH'ING YUEN
WHO IS SAID TO BE 250 YEARS OLD

Once, when Li Ch'ing Yuen was collecting herbs, he met another herbalist who could walk much more quickly than he. Of course, Li Ch'ing Yuen wanted to know how this man could move so fast. The herbalist told him that every day he ate one-third ounce of an herb called *Lycium chinense*. Li Ch'ing Yuen began doing the same, and he became much more vigorous. He married fourteen times successively, and lived to see one hundred and eighty descendants covering eleven generations.

At the age of one hundred and thirty, while traveling in the K'ung-Tung mountains, Li Ch'ing Yuen met a Taoist who was 500 years old. Li Ch'ing Yuen asked the old Taoist the secret of his longevity, and the Taoist taught him an exercise called Ba-Kua (eight trigrams) exercise, which is similar to T'ai Chi Ch'uan.

During his long life, Li Ch'ing Yuen had various occupations. He served as a soldier, sold medicinal herbs, and taught many disciples in the Oh-Mei mountains, Szechuan province. Many of his disciples were over a hundred years old. Some of the oldest men of the district could recall stories their grandfathers had told them about Li Ch'ing Yuen. Even at two hundred and forty-eight years of age, Master Li had good eyesight and a quick stride.

In 1927 General Yang Shen heard about the longevity of this marvelous man and invited Master Li to visit his seat of command in Wan-Shien. He later described Master Li in a book:

> He can walk very quickly in the mountains, even though he's almost 250 years old. He is seven feet tall. His complexion is ruddy, but he is completely bald. His fingernails are very long. In one meal he eats three bowls of rice, chicken, and another kind of meat.

Master Li told Yang Shen that sometimes, while he was in the mountains collecting herbs, his provisions would run out. He would survive by eating herbs, especially ginseng (*Panax schinseng*), *Polygonatum multiflorum,* and *Polygonatum giganteum* var.

Toward the end of his life, Master Li allowed himself to

be photographed. Because of his fame, the eight-inch photo found a ready market. Yang Shen's envoy presented one of these photographs to Generalissimo Chiang Kai-shek, who asked to meet Master Li, but by the time Yang Shen located him, Master Li had died. *The New York Times* reported the death of this wonderful man in 1930.

In 1808, when Master Li Ch'ing Yuen was 130 years old, he traveled to Kansu province, to the sacred K'ung tung mountain. There he met an old Taoist master who claimed to have been born in 1270 A.D. When Master Li asked the ancient Taoist to teach him the secrets of his longevity, the master taught him the exercises which follow in this chapter.

Master Li did these exercises every day for 120 years. They are very effective if done regularly, correctly, and with sincerity. They are best done between 11:00 p.m. and 11:00 a.m. They are most effective if repeated between two and six times. In the beginning, start the exercises slowly. As you become accustomed to them, they will flow smoothly. You should sit in a flat area, on a thick mat or blanket, facing east if possible. At times you will experience gas from the stomach, but this will disappear with practice.

In Master Li's time these exercises were already popular in Chinese society. They are described in the Taoist classics, and several books have been published about them.

The Longevity Exercises

1. Sit on a cushion or thick rug which is comfortable for you. Sit in the lotus position if possible; otherwise try to sit in the half-lotus position or just cross your legs. Taoists always strive to discover the position most comfortable and natural for the body. Relax your shoulders, straighten your back, do not lean. Never strain.
2. Close your eyes and empty your mind. This is difficult because the mind is full of many things. Try to diminish your thoughts. This will help you to see yourself inside.
3. Clench your fists tightly and place them on the thighs close to the knees. Place the fists palms up. This will help to clear thoughts from the mind and enable you to concentrate on the experience of inner energy.

4. Click your teeth together thirty-six times. Do it lightly at a slow, even pace. This can reduce the fever of the heart.

5. With fingers interlocking, place hands palms down on the back of the head. Palms should cover the ears, and the fingers should touch the base of the skull. Place the thumbs below the ears. Gently apply pressure with the palms. Relax your shoulders. This exercise will warm the ears and benefit the kidneys. If your mind is quiet, you will feel the beat of your pulse.

6. Breathe gently and slowly without sound nine times. Think of each breath as energy rising from the heel up to the head. When you exhale allow the energy to fall from your head to the "seat of breathing," below the abdomen. In the words of the Taoist philosopher Chuang Tze:

Concentrate on the goal of meditation.
Do not listen with your ear but listen with your mind;
Not with your mind but with your breath.
Let hearing stop with your ear,

Let the mind stop with its images.
Breathing means to empty oneself and to wait for Tao.
Tao abides only in the emptiness.
This emptiness is the fasting mind...
Look at the void! In it chamber light is produced.
Lo! Joy is here to stay.[1]

7. Place both hands behind the head at the base of the skull. Cover the ears tightly with the palms. Vigorously and quickly beat the index fingers against the base of the skull, at ear level. Alternating the left and the right fingers, beat twenty-four times with each finger (altogether forty-eight times). This exercise will stimulate the brain, prevent deafness and many illnesses, and help one to achieve longevity. It is called Beating the Heavenly Drum.

[1] Chang Chung-Yuan, *Creativity and Taoism* (New York: Julian Press, 1963), p. 129.

8. With fists open or clenched, on the thighs, turn your upper body from right to left. Turn from your waist and

try to coordinate the movement of your head, neck, and shoulders with the waist. Do this forty-eight times, gently, with your eyes open. In Taoist yoga, the neck and upper spinal cords constitute the Heavenly Pillar. This exercise employs the same idea as the T'ai Chi Ch'uan form Waving Hands Like Clouds.

9. Remaining in the same position, run your tongue along the inside of the gums. Begin from left to right along the jaw, then from right to left along the palate. The motion of your tongue will be circular. Do this slowly eighteen times in each direction. Do not swallow the saliva. This exercise is called Red Dragon (tongue) Waves the Water.

10. Your mouth is now full of saliva. Suck the saliva back and forth from the tip of the tongue to the root of the tongue and back to the tip. Do this thirty-six times. Taoists call this saliva the juice of jade.

11. Divide the saliva into three portions. Swallow each portion separately with a vigorous gulp, sending it

straight to your abdomen. The three portions represent
heaven, earth, and man. This can put man in harmony
with his spirit, balance his yin and yang forces, and
increase his vitality. Here is a description from Taoist
yoga of this act of swallowing:

> With the tip of my tongue touching the palate, the two
> glands secreted plentiful saliva and my mouth was soon full
> of it; it was sweet like honey and went down at one gulp
> causing my lower abdomen to vibrate strongly.[2]

When you swallow, listen to the sound of the saliva in
the belly. It can sound like thunder! Taoists explain this
phenomenon thus:

> Straighten your neck and swallow it (saliva). It will then
> enter the channel of function (*jen mo*) to reach the cavity of
> vitality (below the navel) where it will change into negative
> and positive generative force.[3]

[2] Lu K'wan Yu, *Taoist Yoga* (New York: Samuel Weiser, 1970), p. 45.
[3] *Ibid.*

12. Place the left palm over the right and rub the palms in a circular motion from left to right twenty-four times. Then place the right palm over the left and repeat again twenty-four times. This will stimulate circulation and benefit the kidneys. In acupuncture, the palm is an important area:

> First locate the dragon cavity by bending the middle finger of your left hand and where it touches the left palm is that cavity which is lively and is linked with the heart and lower abdomen by a channel (artery) passing through the left wrist. Then locate the tiger cavity by bending the middle finger of your right hand and where it touches the right palm is that cavity which is also linked with the heart and lower abdomen by a channel (vein) passing through the right wrist.[4]

[4] *Ibid.*, p.116

13. Your hands are now warm. Place both hands palms down on the lower back above the kidneys. Vigorously rotate both hands on your back twenty-four times. Then hold them over the kidneys for a few minutes. This will warm and stimulate the activity of the kidneys and increase vitality. This area of the body is called the Gate of Life.

14. Rest your hands on the thighs with fists clenched. Breathe in. Holding your breath, feel the air being drawn into the lower abdomen. Imagine that the breath is like a friendly fire, warming the navel region. When you feel this warmth, breathe out. This part of the body is very important. If the navel region is warm, many diseases will be prevented and energy increased. The Chinese say that if this area is warm, one is half-way to immortality.

15. Extend your left arm out to the side, bending at the
elbow. Rotate the arm in a circular motion going in a
counter-clockwise direction thirty-six times. Repeat
with the right arm. This stimulates the yang yu and yin
yu channels in the Chinese system of acupuncture:

> The yang yu or positive arm channels in the outer sides of
> both arms link both shoulders with the centers of the palms
> after passing through the middle fingers; the yin yu or
> negative arm channels in the inner sides of both arms link
> the centers of the palms with the chest.[5]

[5] *Ibid.*

16. From the crossed-leg position, slowly stretch your legs
out in front of you. Clasp both hands together and raise
your arms above your head, turning the palms outward. Lower the arms, returning the hands to your lap,
turning the palms inward. Do this slowly nine times.

17. Place your palms on the sides of the legs, just below the hips. Slowly stretch your legs out in front. Simultaneously, slide your palms along the outside of your legs. Bend your body forward and allow the head to follow. When the legs and arms are fully extended, grasp the soles of the feet from the outside. Release the feet, sit in an upright position. Repeat 12 times. This exercise is especially good for women because it will firm the thighs and calves and make their legs straight and beautiful.

18. Cross your legs again. Clench your fists tightly and place them on your legs; look straight ahead. Repeat exercises 9, 10, 11. Practice swallowing saliva three times: each time three swallows, altogether nine swallows. When you finish, clench your hands tightly without breathing. Concentrate your mind and let your whole body get very hot. After this you can repeat the exercises from number 4. You can do them three to six times, or as many as you have time for.

CHAPTER THREE
EXCESS AND ITS ANTIDOTES

According to Chinese medical classics, every kind of excess is injurious to one of the inner functions: sleep to the breath, staring to the sperm, sitting to the pulse, standing to the bone, walking to the ligaments, thinking to the spleen, grieving to the heart, lamenting to the lungs, fear to the kidneys, speaking to the saliva, and sexual indulgence to the bone marrow.

Disabilities and malfunctioning of inner organs are the cause of many ailments. Since they have their origins inside the body, people are often unaware of them and tend to ignore them when the ailment is slight and does not pose any immediate problem. However, it is a universal medical fact that prevention is much easier than cure. The exercises in this chapter will help maintain or restore the health of the inner organs.

THE "SIX SOUNDS" THERAPY

Traditional Chinese medicine uses several ways to prevent or curb diseases. One of them is a method called "the six sounds" therapy, which is used by Taoists and Buddhists alike. The six sounds are *HA, HU, SHI, SSSSS, SHU, FU.* These sounds are to be pronounced as much as possible in an aspirated or sibilant way; for instance the sound *FU* is to be uttered as if one were blowing a fire. Each sound cures a particular ailment and is beneficial to a specific inner organ: *HA* is beneficial to the heart, *HU* to the spleen, *SSSSS* to the lungs, *SH* to the solar plexus, *SHU* to the liver, and *FU* to the kidneys. If the heart needs healing, the patient places his hands, fingers intertwined, behind his head and utters the sound *HA* thirty-six times. For kidneys, the sound *FU* is pronounced thirty-six times while the patient sits on the floor, arms around his knees, hands clasped. For the liver the procedure is the same as for the heart, except that the sound *SHU* is pronounced thirty-six times. For the lungs, the patient stands with hands held together behind him while he utters the sound *SSSSS* thirty-six times. For the spleen the hands are held over the stomach and the sound *HU* is pronounced thirty-six times. If the stomach feels hot or feverish, the patient lies down on his back, closes his eyes, and utters the sound SHU thirty-six times.

Even if you do not suffer from any ailment, the daily practice of these exercises can be very beneficial to the inner organs.

HEALING METHODS WITH THE EYES

Staring at a crystal ball is a traditional Chinese method of curing disabilities of the inner organs. The patient opens his eyes wide and watches a crystal ball held seven or eight inches from the eyes. Breathing deeply and audibly, he watches closely until tears appear; he then closes his eyes and practices gentle breathing in quiet, meditative concentration. The exercise is then repeated. The gentle breathing with eyes closed lasts twice as long as the audible breathing with eyes open.

Rolling the eyes is beneficial to the health of the inner organs as well as the eyes themselves. Roll the eyes from left to right (clockwise), that is, from A to B to C to D; this movement is combined with breathing in. Breathing out is simultaneous with rolling the eyes from C to D to A to B.

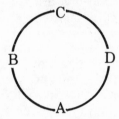

The clockwise motion is carried out nine times, during which the tongue may follow the direction and movement of the eyes. Then stop, close the eyes, and practice gentle breathing, while the mind is in a relaxed meditative state. Then start the first nine rounds again, followed by closed eyes and relaxed mind. This is done for four rounds thirty-six times.

In the second part, the procedure is repeated, except that the movement is counter-clockwise and that, instead of nine times, each exercise is made of six complete circles (altogether twenty-four times).

SQUATTING

This meditative exercise is best done at night, with the windows open, before going to bed.

Covering your ears with the palms of your hands, sit in a squatting position; hold your upper body erect. If you find the position difficult at the beginning, lean against the side of a bed, couch, or similar object.

The squatting posture is modeled on the fetus in the womb. Just as the unborn baby, with eyes, ears, and mouth closed, is in a state of quiet inactivity, so, too, the individual meditating in squatting posture is in a calm state, devoid of postnatal cares and distractions. He returns, as it were to the origin. In the words of Lao Tze, "Things appear multifarious and plural, but eventually they all return to the common root; when they return to the common root there is quiescence."

Squatting is at once a meditation and an exercise. As an exercise, it facilitates digestion, strengthens the leg muscles, and helps straighten the spinal cord, so that the inner organs work with ease and efficiency.

Whether squatting is done as exercise or meditation, breathing is quite important. In the beginning you can inhale and exhale through the nose; breathe slowly and deeply, with attention focused on the lower abdomen. After a certain time, when enough quiescence has been achieved, you may be able to do the kind of deep, quiet breathing known to Taoists as heel breathing. It is at this stage that you become attuned to the normally inaudible workings of your body; actually hearing, with closed ears, your inner rhythms.[1]

SWALLOWING AIR

Many people in the affluent societies of the West suffer from overweight. In the United States dieting has become a national preoccupation and a major industry.

---

[1] Yang-Shen, *Biography of a 250-Year-Old-Man* (Taiwan: World Publishing Co., 1970).

Maintaining an attractive figure is the main motivation for the majority of dieters, but overweight is a serious medical problem as well. It is linked with a variety of heart ailments and cardiac disabilities.

The chief difficulty with dieting is that abstinence from food causes physical discomfort, so that the individual, with all his good intentions, resorts to eating.

The physical discomfort of hunger is caused by the self-grinding of the stomach in the absence of food. A simple, effective method to alter this condition is to swallow air. Since the stomach is an inflatable organ, the air expands it like a rubber ball; the grinding of the interior of the stomach ceases, and the hunger pain stops.

The ancient Taoists used this method not only for temporary toleration of hunger in the absence of food, but also as an aid to health and rejuvenation. Air is believed to contain a good deal of healing properties, and swallowing air is referred to in Taoist classics as ingestion of heaven and earth.

MEDITATIVE BREATHING

There are two kinds of breathing. Outer breathing is the common activity of inhaling and exhaling through the nose or mouth. Inner breathing is a subtler and more advanced form; in Taoist classics it is called embryo or fetus breathing. At the highest level of inner breathing, the individual may reach perfect psychophysical harmony when respiration seems to have ceased altogether. This is called the great quiescence.

That the Taoists, at this stage, are said to have reached immortality is not difficult to understand. Being the indispensible activity for all sentient beings, breathing stops when life comes to an end. It follows that with the

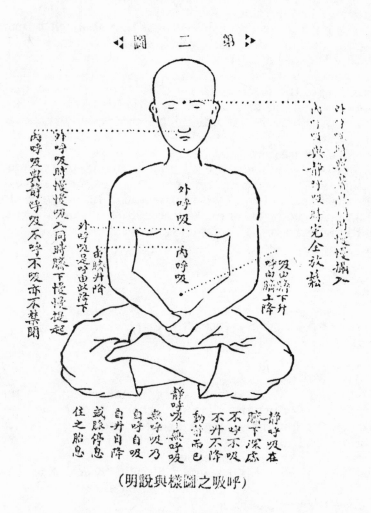

◄ 圖 二 第 ►

外呼吸與靜呼吸同時慢慢攝入

內呼吸與靜呼吸時完全放鬆

外呼吸　內呼吸

吸由臍下上升
呼由臍上降

內呼吸與靜呼吸不呼不吸亦不禁閉

外呼吸時慢慢吸入同時膝下慢慢提起

由臍升降

外呼吸是呼由此降

靜呼吸在
臍下深處
不呼不吸
不升不降
動靜而已

靜呼吸，無呼吸
照呼吸乃
自呼自吸
自升自降
或脈停息
住之胎息

（明說與樣圖之吸呼）

prior cessation of breathing in the great quiescence no longer does this cause-and-effect process hold true.

Meditative breathing is best carried out in a clean, tidy room with a window open. One should sit on something soft and comfortable, yet firm and unsagging. A board bed or a low bench covered with a cushion or blanket would be ideal.

The best time to practice is in the evening before going to bed—the time of rest and tranquillity. The Taoists call it the time of *tze* (11:00 p.m. to 1:00 a.m.), when outside is yin and inside the root of yang is just beginning to sprout. The corresponding time of year is midwinter, when the surface of the earth is covered with snow, trees and plants have died, and animals are at rest or hibernating, but beneath the surface of the soil, plants and animals are beginning to come to life.

People who suffer from insomnia are advised to practice meditation breathing at the evening hours of *tze* as a relaxing preparation for sleep. Morning meditation is also desirable as after a night's sleep the body and the mind are refreshed and alert.

Meditative breathing starts with outer breathing. Sitting comfortably in half-lotus position, hands on the lap, head straight, put the tongue against the palate and half-close your eyes. Air is inhaled through the nostrils and, to facilitate the expulsion of dirty air, exhaled through the mouth. The mind is centered at the point between the eyes and behind them.

The air from the nose is breathed down as far as the abdomen, below the navel; at the same time, prenatal breathing pushes the breath (*ch'i*) from the base of the genitals to below the navel. Thus postnatal and prenatal breathing meet at the same point, bringing "the fire and water together."

When exhaling, the air is expelled through the mouth and nose and, at the same time, the *ch'i* descends from the lower abdomen back to the base of the genitals. By repeating the deep, regular breathing in this manner, plenty of oxygen-rich air accumulates in the lower abdomen; since oxygen kindles fire, the abdominal area feels warm. In the words of the Taoist classics, "the fire dwells in the water place." This process is believed to prevent a variety of diseases by making excess water evaporate. In addition, the fire thus kindled helps the various substances in the abdominal area undergo chemical transmutations, whereby body metabolism reaches its optimal function and vitality is increased.

At the second stage, the concentration on the point between the eyes is released, and the breathing is reduced to inner breathing, which, without the conscious will of the meditator, is carried out by the mere movement of the *ch'i* itself, whose direction is now from the heart downward to the abdomen and from the base of the genitals upward to the same abdominal area.

TAOIST JOGGING

Taoist jogging is a form of deliberate meditation-exercise, in its outward form not unlike the American jogging. In Chinese it is called *shieng chio*, "walking with high strides." In classical Taoist texts there is reference to dragon *shieng chio*, reindeer *shieng chio* and tiger *shieng chio*, indicating the different animals which the individual represents in his meditative jogging. In traditional *shieng chio* preparatory aids and activities such as magic rituals, meat-free diet or complete fasting, and ablutions were carried out.

Shieng chio as a form of meditative exercise dispels such emotions as sadness, anger, and pensiveness. For this purpose it is a more workable method than sitting meditation, as the latter can be conducive to increased thinking and ideation.

Walking aids the free circulation of blood and increases

the intake of fresh air—particularly beneficial if the walking is carried out in the country—giving the body access to more oxygen. Moreover, exercising the body in an ever-changing spectacle of nature calms the mind and invigorates the spirit, so that gradually one ceases to identify himself with the body or be distracted by outside circumstances. Thus one reaches a state of awareness in which body and mind—and nature at large—coalesce into one entity. This is the Tao.

It is different from ordinary walking as well as American jogging which, characteristically, confines itself to the awkward and superficial exterior, ignoring the underlying subtleties. In *shieng chio,* as in T'ai Chi Ch'uan and other Taoist activities, the human body can be compared, in modern terms, to an automobile. It is not just the wheels which make the automobile run, nor the fuel, nor the driver alone. All three are indispensible for smooth, speedy operation.

In meditative long-stride walking, the driver is the mind, the fuel is the breathing *(ch'i)* and the wheels are the arms and legs.

1. Eyes should look straight ahead. This helps keep the mind directed forward, hence calm, and the body balanced.
2. Tongue should be held against the palate. This reinforces the effect of being directed forward; it also promotes the secretion of saliva, which prevents thirst and provides nourishment.
3. The head and body should be erect, shoulders relaxed, arms naturally hanging down and moving freely.
4. Place the mind and breathing *(ch'i)* in the area of *tan t'ien,* one and one-third inches below the navel, at the body's center of gravity.
5. The foot which takes the step should be a little higher than in normal walking, although not too high.
6. The whole body should be relaxed, joints and muscles included, so that one can feel quite light and nimble.

The best time for Taoist jogging is in the morning, but if

work makes this impossible, evening is all right. The time period should be very short in the beginning and increased gradually to one to three hours.

The exercise should be carried out every day. A feeling of tiredness is normal in the beginning; it will disappear as you become more relaxed and nimble. Like an automobile or a windmill, once the momentum is gained, you can coast along without much additional fuel. You will begin to feel vitality *(ch'i)* gathering in the lower abdomen, later filling the entire body. The legs begin to move smoothly, lightly, like the wheels of an automobile. A pleasant sensation of tingling warmth is felt in the hands. Gradually you forget that you are actually performing the act of walking.

Still a better analogy can be made with swimming. A beginning swimmer uses much effort and energy; an accomplished swimmer finds the water actually helping him. He swims without getting tired and can float on water. In a similar way, the individual proficient in walking exercise feels his body lighter than the air. Leih Tzu calls this kind of jogging Riding on the Wind; in Chinese martial arts it is called Flying on the Land. It has been compared to the flight of the swallow; in fact, the martial artist Li Shan is nicknamed "the Swallow."

Taoists use this exercise as an aid in meditative "immortality." They were particularly fond of it in ancient times, when wandering without a destination ("traveling like clouds") was quite popular.

Master Li, the celebrated 250-year-old herbalist, seems to have achieved a similar competence in walking. He attained such agility and quickness that he wasn't afraid of wild animals.

A similar proficiency in walking and moving is attributed to Master Chang San Feng, the creator of T'ai Chi Ch'uan, who was often said to have been seen in the evening hundreds of miles away from where he had been seen in the morning. To paraphrase the *I Ching,* only through the Tao can one go fast without hurrying and reach the goal as if without moving.

THE ANIMAL EXERCISES OF HWA T'O

TIGER   BEAR

MONKEY   DEER   BIRD

In about the third century A.D., Hwa T'o, a Chinese medical doctor and an excellent surgeon, devised a very effective method for operating on internal organs and on external wounds.

Observing that "flowing water never stagnates" and that a used door step never splits apart, he invented an exercise called the Movement of the Five Animals, to stimulate the circulation of the blood, relax the joints, and relax the muscles of the body.

The first exercise is the Tiger, in which the body is stretched forward from the waist and the arms and legs are stretched as well. The second is the Bear, in which the head is moved slowly from side to side. The third is the Monkey, in which the hands hold on to a bar and the arms lift up the whole body. The fourth is the Deer, in which the head is dropped to the chest and the legs are drawn up to the chest in a crouching position. The fifth is the Bird, in which the arms move like wings and the legs are lifted and waved about as in swimming.

These exercises complete and augment the Tao Yin.

T'AI CHI CH'UAN

The T'ai Chi Ch'uan, a detailed system of slow, flowing, and subtly configurated motions, is a relaxing and tonifying exercise whose physiotherapeutic benefits are numerous.

In contemporary China T'ai Chi is carried out as daily exercises by people of all ages and both sexes. Its popularity among Americans increased greatly after President Nixon's trip to China.

More than a popular physical exercise, T'ai Chi Ch'uan is a bona fide adjunct to medical therapy in many hospitals, sanitariums, and convalescent homes. One of my students, a psychiatrist and the director of a hospital, and a group of medical doctors, organized a medical treatment center in Rockland County, New York; they use T'ai Chi Ch'uan and Chinese meditation along with western techniques as a therapy for their patients' convalescence.

It is used in a number of drug rehabilitation centers, especially in New York and California.

Cases and examples attesting to T'ai Chi Ch'uan's success in curbing and curing physical and mental malfunctioning, and as an aid to longevity, are numerous. Li Chou Ch'ien, a devotee and master of T'ai Chi Ch'uan, was ninety years old when I met him in China. He was youthful in appearance and had remarkable vision, being able to read extremely small print without glasses.

Liu Yao-Ting, another T'ai Chi master, took up the exercise at age sixty, after a heart attack. Today, in his middle eighties, he is a healthy and vigorous teacher of T'ai Chi. A similar case, Dr. Wang Huai Ming, is eighty-three years old. A former assistant of mine in New York City's YWCA, Dr. Wang now continues to teach the art independently.

The following pages do not by any means exhaust the different forms of T'ai Chi Ch'uan; they merely represent a few basic forms. For a complete description and illustration of all the forms, the reader is urged to consult a reliable book on T'ai Chi Ch'uan.

The forms of the first section (shown here) of T'ai Chi Ch'uan are fairly easy to learn and practice. The more advanced forms, such as Snake Creeps Down and Golden Cock Stands on One Leg, are more difficult. For health purposes the first section is adequate; for self-defense, as well as health, the second part is more useful, but requires more time and interest on the part of the student.

In order to begin to realize the harmony of the body and mind, old ingrained habits must be unlearned and new habits formed. This takes a degree of concentration and should be given time and practice to manifest itself. A new shoot on an old tree is delicate and must be allowed to develop at its own pace. This is one of the central lessons of T'ai Chi Ch'uan.

The beginning of the T'ai Chi brings the vital flow up from the yang (large intestine) meridian channels (from

the tips of the fingers to the ears); the downward movement of the hands and body involves the yin (heart)
meridian (from the armpit to the ends of the fingers).
Chuang Tze states: "The common people breathe with
their throats, while the perfect man breathes with his
heel."

In Grasp Bird's Tail, the second movement, turn the
body to the right (yin), then left (yang); then push up, pull
back, press forward, push forward. This is comparable to
the four seasons. Completing the first section thus completes the whole function of heaven and earth.

1. Stand, hands easily to your sides, palms facing
   backwards.
2. Check your bodily alignment. Imagine a line from the
   crown of your head through your spine to your heels.
   Drop your shoulders; feel the body as though it were
   hanging on the spine, the knees and legs without
   tension.
3. Relax your mind toward the gravity center of the body,
   two inches below the navel, and return to this gravity
   center whenever the mind wanders.
4. Place the tip of the tongue lightly against the palate.
5. Lighten the body. Feel as children do when playing,
   and "play" the forms.

Playing the Forms

1. The heels are together, toes slightly outward. Put the
   weight onto the right foot and separate the feet,
   moving the left foot to the side, toes straight forward.
   Move the weight to the left foot; straighten the toes of
   the right foot by pivoting them forward on the heel.
   The weight is evenly distributed over both feet.
2. Allow the arms to rise upward in front of you, elbows,
   wrists, and fingers without tension. At shoulder height,
   slightly straighten the fingers and draw your wrists
   toward your shoulders and press your hands down to
   where they began—easily along your sides.
   Note: This is a circular movement.

74

Grasp Bird's Tail

1. Shift the weight to the left leg.
2. All together, turn body (and head along with it) slightly to the right and lift the toes of the right foot; pivoting on the heel, let the foot turn with the body. The arms rise, the right above the left, as though holding an invisible ball.

3. Move your weight onto the right leg, slightly turn your body and head forward again, step with your left foot a little to the left and slightly forward—heel first—the toes straight forward, the knee always over the foot, not bent inward. As your weight moves forward, the left hand moves up to your chin level and slightly in front of you. As though a string connects the left hand and the right toes, the moving left hand draws the right toes inward a little. The pelvis faces straight ahead and is not twisted. The right arm returns to the side.

Push Up

1. The weight moves almost all to the left foot, freeing the right foot to pivot on the toe as the body and head turn to the right. The right hand pivots palm forward with the pivoting foot.
2. Step a little to the right and slightly forward; heel first, toes straight forward.
3. Simultaneously, the right hand moves upward and directly in front of you, the invisible string pulling the left toes inward; the left hand presses forward, moving toward the right palm.
4. The weight moves forward.
5. The pelvis faces directly forward.

Pull Back

1. Turn both palms over (the left upward toward the right, which faces downward toward the left). Both hands move diagonally a little upward toward the right corner; as though holding something between them they fall naturally downward, diagonally across the body to the left. The falling is as water flows downward, effortlessly and uncontrived. The torso moves slightly sideways to the left.
2. Simultaneously, the weight shifts backward onto the left bent leg. Do not throw the hip out of line. The weight shifts onto the bending leg and draws the arms backwards.

Press Forward

1. The left forearm circles naturally backward, the palm remaining forward, and returns, pressing forward at the height of the ear.
2. It presses forward toward the right palm, which rises up as before, directly in front of the body.
3. The weight moves onto the right bent leg.

Separate Hands, Sit Back

1. Separate the hands to shoulder width.
2. The weight shifts backward onto the left bent leg and draws the body over the knee, the arms toward the body at shoulder height, the elbows and shoulders very relaxed.

Press Forward

1. The body weight moves forward; with the arms in the same easy position, press forward.

Single Whip

1. Move the weight back, leave the arms where they are. This will slightly straighten them.
2. Lift the right toes and pivot on the heel, and, as though the arms and feet could only move together, turn the body left around toward the front until the right foot and arms will turn no more.

3. Shift the weight onto the right bent leg, and, simultaneously, turn the body toward the left; pivot on the left toes, move the left arm across your body, palm up and slightly below the navel height, and move the right arm out to the side, fingers bent toward the thumb as though holding someone's wrist.

4. Step, heel first, to the left. The step is wide, accomplishing a quarter turn from your beginning direction. The knees are bent.
5. As the weight moves forward, the left hand turns and presses forward in front of you, as though your fingertips are pressing toward something. The invisible string between the left hand and the right foot pulls the right toes inward.

CHAPTER FOUR
ACUPUNCTURE

Traditional Chinese medicine in general and acupuncture in particular are based on the law of Tao and on the yin-yang principle. Just as the interaction of opposites—light and dark, heaven and earth, hard and soft, and so on— govern the life of the universe, so too the human body, the universe in miniature, functions in a minutely configured yin-yang balance. What is called disease is the disturbance of this balance. It follows, then, that the healing process, as well as the prevention of disease, involves the restoration and maintenance of this balance.

Acupuncture is a method by which the energy of the body is regulated and brought into balance through the manipulation of certain key points on the surface of the body. These points are acted upon in several ways: they are principally used to act on the major organs, to tonify where there is a deficiency of energy, and to sedate where there is an excess.

The number of points used in acupuncture have not always been the same. The *Nei Ching*, the oldest Chinese medical book, gives 365 points, equivalent to the number of days in a year. Later acupuncturists have added to this figure. Today there are approximately a thousand.

The points lie on the route of external paths called meridians. There are twelve basic meridians, which take their names from and correspond to the twelve inner organs.

The meridians are pathways of energy at the surface of the body. They are connected to the internal organs by intermediate circulatory paths. Acupuncture influences the core circulation and balance of the body through manipulation of this surface circulatory system.

八卦干支十二屬象圖

CHART OF THE CHINESE YEARS IN THE TWELVE ANIMAL CYCLE

YEAR OF HORSE
1966 WU 1978

YEAR OF SHEEP
1967 WEI 1979

YEAR OF SERPENT
1977 SSU 1989

YEAR OF MONKEY
1968 SHEN 1980

YEAR OF DRAGON
1976 CH'EN 1988

YEAR OF COCK
1969 YU 1981

YEAR OF RABBIT
1975 MAO 1987

YEAR OF DOG
1970 HSU 1982

YEAR OF TIGER
1974 YEN 1986

YEAR OF PIG
1971 HAI 1983

YEAR OF OX
1973 CH'OU 1985

YEAR OF RAT
1972 TZU 1984

88

The meridians lie on both sides of the body. On each meridian there are a number of types of points, which include the *tonification point, sedation point,* and *source point.* The meridians follow a fixed order, and are classified as yin or yang. The yin meridians are primarily related to organs which can be characterized as having primarily storage functions, while the yang meridians are characterized as active, working organs. The yin organs are the lungs, spleen, kidneys, and liver. The yang organs are the large intestine, stomach, small intestine, bladder, and gall bladder.

The yin-yang principle pervades all acupuncture philosophy and practice. Each organ and meridian has a yin or yang designation. Every treatment process begins with a diagnostic analysis by the practitioner of the general and specific character of the patient's functioning. Treatment is given according to the need for increasing or decreasing energy to certain parts of the body; that is, for tonification or sedation action, according to certain basic laws of acupuncture.

The principle diagnostic technique in acupuncture treatment is the taking of the pulse. In contrast to Western medicine, this is an involved, refined, and highly skilled practice. Since acupuncture was passed on for generations through the family in China, the techniques were acquired very early in life.

The pulse is generally taken on the radial artery of each arm. Each hand contains six pulses of major organs. These can be felt in three positions by placing the first three fingers on the radial artery below the palm. They are found at a superficial level and a deep level. On the left hand is found the pulses of the small intestine, gall bladder, bladder, heart, liver, and kidneys. On the right hand is found the pulses of the large intestine, stomach, triple warmer, lungs, spleen, and the heart governor organs. There is a rule of balance operating between each hand as well. This is the rule that the left hand always rules the

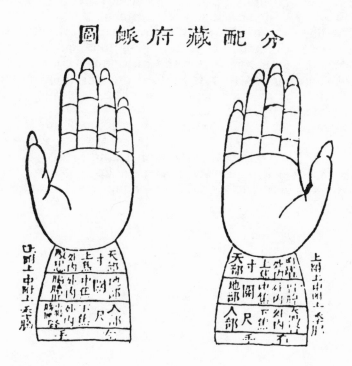

right hand to maintain a proper balance. This relationship has its basis in the five elements law. The yin organ pulses are found at the deep level, the yang organ pulses at the superficial level.

There are several operational laws involved in acupuncture practice. These laws state the direct and indirect relationships between meridians, organs, and channels of the body. The five elements law is considered the most important; it is essentially a theory of relationships in the universe in general and in the physical system in particular.

Left Hand   Right Hand

First position

superficial: small intestine   superficial: large intestine
deep: heart   deep: lungs

Second position

superficial: gall bladder   superficial: stomach
deep: liver   deep: spleen

Third position

superficial: bladder   superficial: triple warmer
deep: kidneys   deep: heart governor

The five elements, wood, fire, earth, metal, and water, are not thought of as concrete things, but as processes operating in nature. They are stages through which the flow of energy passes, and which express that energy in particular ways, just as water may be liquid, solid, or gas. This relationship is shown in the diagram.

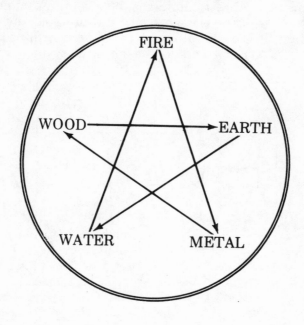

Wood	liver	gall bladder
Fire	heart	small intestine
Earth	spleen	stomach
Metal	lungs	large intestine
Water	kidneys	bladder

The organs can be classified by elements as shown in the table.

As can be seen on the diagram, there are two basic flows of energy among the five elements. The circular, outer flow is the positive, helping flow, called the father-mother-son cycle. The inner cycle is the destructive negative cycle. According to the five elements law, tonification of a wood organ also tonifies a fire organ, while sedating an earth organ. Tonification occurs according to the creative father-mother-son cycle, while sedation occurs on the destroyer cycle. The five elements law involves remedying imbalance in the relationship between parts of the system. Each of the five elements is to be found on each meridian; there is a wood, earth, metal, fire, and water point on each meridian, which, when stimulated, acts according to the five elements law. It involves invigorating areas where there are deficiencies and sedating areas where there is excess energy.

Among the several factors to be taken into account in acupuncture treatment are the universal rhythms: time of day and season. Energy flows through the body in a regular rhythm according to the five elements law, from wood, to fire, to earth, to metal, to water, in a twenty-four hour cycle. The heart is at its highest energy peak at noon, its lowest at midnight. This cycle will affect the tonification or sedation of an organ, and adjustments are made according to this fact.

The moxa technique associated with acupuncture is one of the more important forms of herbal therapy. It involves cauterizing by burning an herb, usually the dried leaf of *Artemesia* (mugwort), on the acupuncture point. The herb is placed on a given point and burned until the patient feels it is too hot and before a burn occurs, and then is rapidly removed. Thin cakes of ginger or ju are also used above the acupuncture point.

THE EIGHT PSYCHIC CHANNELS

Vital energy moves in the body not only on the peripheral meridians, but through various connective paths which reach every cell in the body. The eight psychic channels both store and transmit energy from the meridians to the deepest organic pathways and between the meridians themselves. Only two of the psychic channels have acupuncture points which lie on their paths. The others are most directly reached through points on the twelve meridians. Excesses and deficiencies of energy along these channels may have a very serious effect on the balance of energy on the body as a whole. These channels generally will absorb the overflow of ch'i from the meridians, and have the capacity to store energy. At certain points in many disorders acting on these channels may be very important.

Of the eight major psychic channels the first two, *Tu Mo* and *Jen Mo*, are the only ones which have acupuncture points.

The *Tu Mo*, or Channel of Control, has twenty-eight points, beginning at the coccyx, traveling up the spine and over the skull, ending at the gum. If this channel is not functioning properly, the sufferer may experience bladder trouble, pain in the lower abdomen or chest, or a hernia. Disorders treated on this meridian include: hemorrhoids, insomnia, nervous disorders, and nasal disorders. Many points on this meridian are used to stimulate and tonify organs in general.

The *Jen Mo*, or Channel of Function, begins at the base of the genitals and travels up the center of the body, ending on the face just above the chin. It connects twenty-four points.

If this channel is not functioning properly, the back of the neck will feel stiff, and there will be spiritual unrest in the person. Disorders which may be affected by acupuncture on this meridian: migraine headaches, asthma, lung disorders, intestinal disorders.

The third channel is the *Tai Mo,* or Belt Channel, and is a belt which passes around both sides of the navel and encircles the belly. If this channel is not functioning the belly is distended, and the waist will feel cold and wet, as though one were sitting in water. Loss of appetite will be another symptom. Disorders involved with this channel: the belly swells out with dropsy, the waist feels cool as in the water.

The fourth channel is called the *Ch'ueng Mo,* or Thrusting Channel, and it goes up from the genitals, between the Jen Mo and the Tu Mo. It ends in the heart. If it is not functioning, disorders of the digestive system will result.

The fifth channel is called the *Yang (Yu) Wei Mo,* or Positive Arm Channel. It rises from below the navel, moves across the chest, and extends down both the inner arms to the palm and middle fingertip. If it is affected, the heart will be aggravated, the palms will feel feverish, muscles in the arm are contracted, and the arm joints are rigid. Disorders: headaches, fever, toothaches.

The sixth channel is the *Yin (Yu) Wei Mo,* or Negative Arm Channel. It passes through the arms, but the emphasis here is on the veins rather than the arteries. Disorders involved on this channel: nervous disorders, epilepsy, hypertension, hemorrhoids.

The seventh and eighth channels are the *Yang Chiao (Mo),* or Positive Leg Channels, and the *Yin Chiao (Mo),* or Negative Leg Channels. The Yang Chiao, the seventh channel, rises from the heel and turns along the outer sides of the ankles and legs, up to the side of the body, around the head, and down below the ear. If it is not functioning properly, the sufferer will be unable to sleep.

The eighth channel, the Yin Chiao, rises from the instep of the foot, up through the inner leg, past the genital organs, up through the center of the body, to a middle spot between the eyebrows. If this is malfunctioning, the sufferer will sleep too much. Yang Chiao: disorders resulting from imbalance or improper functioning, paralysis, lethargy, weakness, etc. Yin Chiao: disorders resulting from insomnia, general disorders.

The base of the eight psychic channels is the Gate of Mortality at the root of the genital organs, which is linked with the base of the spine by the Tu Mo. Following the Tu Mo up the body, it is joined at the brain by the Jen Mo. From the center of the brain, the channel descends down through the center of the head cavity to the palate, the

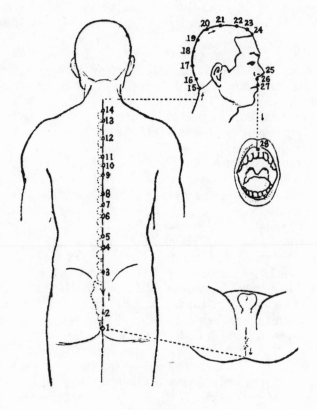

TU MO

Heavenly Pool. The Heavenly Pool is connected to the jawbone, and this system is used in breathing and meditation to allow the *ch'i* to collect and escape. Under the palate, the channel goes down the throat, through the pulmonary artery, down the hepatic artery, past and under the diaphragm, behind the solar plexus, below the navel, and back to the root of the genitals. In other words, the total channel system passes through the body in a circle, starting and ending at the genitals.

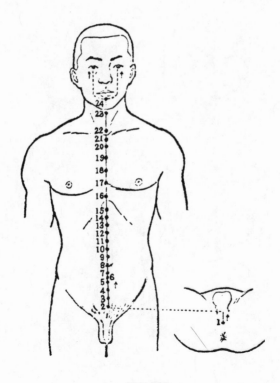

JEN MO

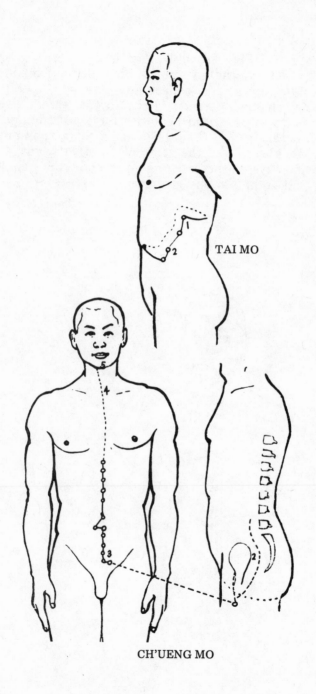

TAI MO

CH'UENG MO

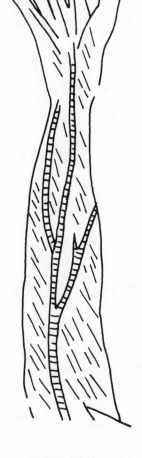

DETAIL FROM
YANG (YU) WEI MO

DETAIL FROM
YIN (YU) WEI MO

YANG CHIAO

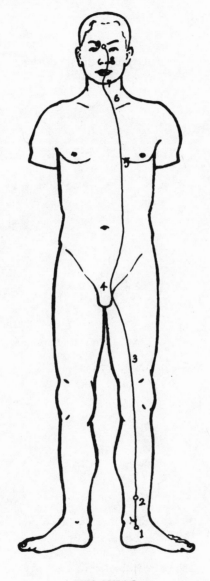

YIN CHIAO

ULTIMATELESSNESS

Compounding the spiritual consciousness back to Nonbeing and returning to the ultimatelessness.

To take K'an ☵ unifying with Li ☲

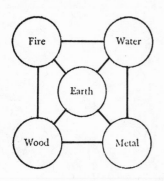

Five breaths assembled at the source

Compounding essence into breath, and compounding breath into spiritual consciousness

The Gate of the Dark Femininity

LUNG MERIDIAN

A yin meridian, the lung meridian is centrifugal in direction. It starts near the armpit, between the second and third ribs, and runs along the upper and lower arms, ending on the inside of the thumb, at the root of the nail. The lung meridian is associated with the element of metal, and has eleven points on each side of the body.

Many of the disorders which can be treated on the lung meridian are respiratory or respiratory-related: asthma, bronchitis; conjunctivitis, coughing, pulmonary disorders, throat disorders. The *ho* point (point 5) is associated with such disorders as chronic anxiety, paralysis, and restlessness.

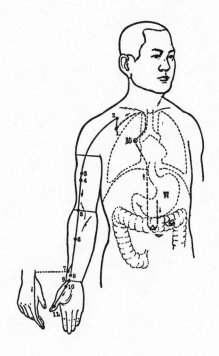

KIDNEY MERIDIAN

The kidney meridian is a yin meridian associated with the water element. It connects twenty-seven points on each side of the body. It is centripetal, beginning on the sole of the foot, traveling up the inside leg to the center of the body, and ending just below the collarbone, between the clavicle and the first rib. Disorders involved with this meridian include stomach disorders, gastritis, liver infections, vomiting, hernia, eye disorders, and genital disorders.

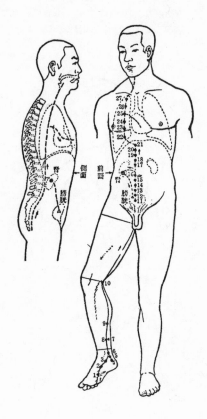

LARGE INTESTINE MERIDIAN

The large intestine meridian is yang in character and associated with the metal element. It connects twenty points on each side of the body. It is a centripetal meridian, beginning at the base of the index fingernail, traveling up the inner side of the arm and ending at the side of the nostril. As its name indicates, this meridian is primarily concerned with conditions of the large intestine, as well as the abdominal region in general. Secondary ailments treated on this meridian are associated with teeth, gums, and a variety of skin diseases. Examples: ulcers, constipation, cramps, stomatitis, tonsilitis, neuralgia, paralysis of various types.

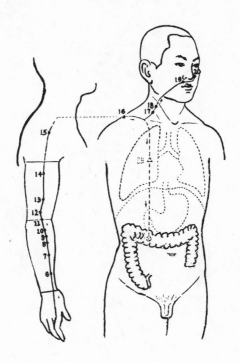

THE SPLEEN MERIDIAN

The spleen meridian is a yin meridian associated with the earth element, connecting twenty-one points on each side of the body. It is centripetal, beginning at the root of the nail of the big toe, continuing up the inside of the leg and torso, and ending below the armpit. Disorders treated on the spleen meridian include gastrointestinal disorders, uterine and ovarian disorders, weakness, exhaustion, insomnia, and bronchitis.

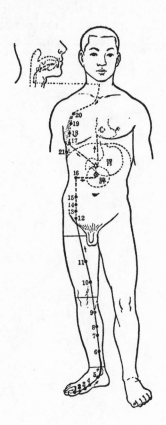

GALL BLADDER MERIDIAN

The gall bladder meridian is yang and is associated with the wood element. It links forty-four points on each side of the body. It is centrifugal, beginning at the outer corner of the eye, traveling around several points on the head, down the side of the body, and ending at the second joint of the fourth toe. Disorders involved with the gall bladder meridian include insomnia, migraine, ear and eye disorders, headaches, hypertension, nose disorders, and fever.

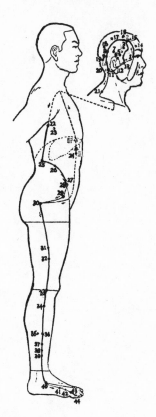

THE TRIPLE WARMER MERIDIAN

The triple warmer meridian is yang in character, and is associated with the fire element. It connects twenty-three points on each side of the body. The first point is on the ring finger, on the little finger side. The meridian is centripetal, traveling up the hand and arm to the head, ending near the eye, under the eyebrow. Disorders related to the triple warmer meridian: constipation, bronchitis, diabetes, deafness, paralysis, arthritis.

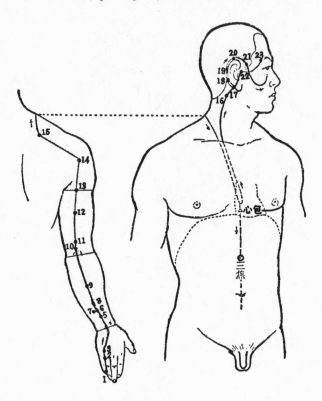

HEART MERIDIAN

The heart meridian is a yin meridian, associated with the fire element. It is centrifugal, connecting nine points on each side of the body, beginning at the base of the armpit and traveling down the inner side of the arm to the base of the little fingernail. Disorders aided by treatment on the heart meridian include psychological and emotional disturbances, anxiety, heart disorders, insomnia.

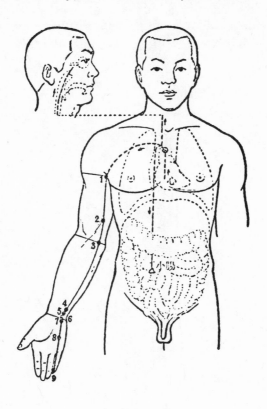

BLADDER MERIDIAN

The bladder meridian is a yang meridian, associated with the water element. It is centrifugal, beginning at the inside corner of the eye, traveling over the skull, down the spinal column, and ending at the base of the little toenail. There are sixty-seven points on each side of the body connected by this meridian. The following are some examples of disorders aided by this meridian: abdominal disorders (especially in children), arthritis, eye disorders, abdominal and intestinal hemorrhaging, hemorrhoids, mouth disorders, ulcers, spasms, throat disorders, paralysis.

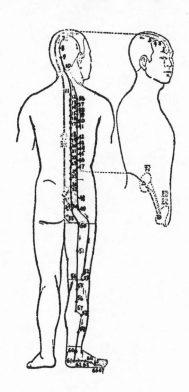

STOMACH MERIDIAN

The stomach meridian is yin in character and is associated with the earth element. It involves forty-five points on each side of the body. The meridian moves centrifugally, beginning just under the eye, moving down the body and legs, and ending at the root of the second toenail. The stomach meridian contains the only acupuncture points on the body which are considered forbidden to any acupuncture treatment. These lie on the main artery system, and at the center of the nipples. Disorders treated on the stomach meridian include all infections of the abdominal organs, eye disorders, mouth disorders, neuralgia, paralysis, and nervous disorders.

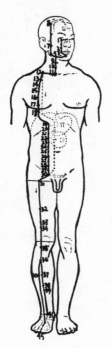

SMALL INTESTINE MERIDIAN

A yang meridian in character, the small intestine meridian is associated with the fire element. It moves in a centripetal direction, beginning at the base of the little fingernail, traveling up the arm and side of the face, and ending at the front of the ear. It connects nineteen points on each side of the body. The points on the small intestine meridian are used in treating a variety of disorders, including arthritis, eye disorders, epilepsy, bronchitis, deafness, and various types of paralysis.

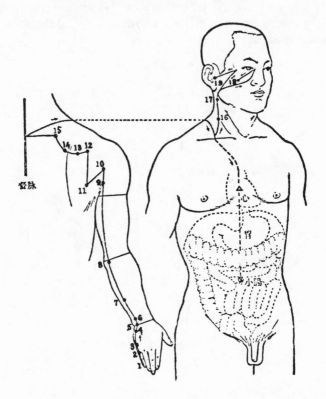

HEART GOVERNER MERIDIAN

This yin meridian, the heart governer meridian, is associated with the fire element, and connects nine points on each side of the body. It begins in the chest-muscle area, traveling centripetally down the arm, ending at the base of the middle fingernail. Examples of disorders which are treated on this meridian: tonsilitis, stomach disorders, nightmares, hemorrhoids.

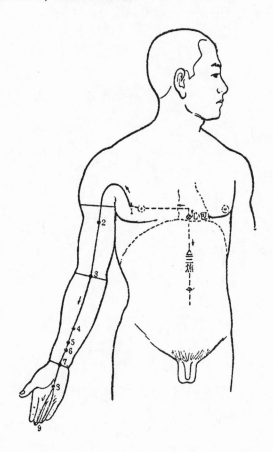

LIVER MERIDIAN

The liver meridian is a yin meridian which travels in a
centrifugal direction. Associated with the wood element, it
starts at the base of the nail of the big toe, travels up the
inside of the leg and thigh and ends near the nipple. The
liver meridian connects fourteen points on each side of the
body. Some of the disorders involved with the liver
meridian: eye disorders, liver and abdominal disorders,
diabetes, colds, arthritis, uterine disorders.

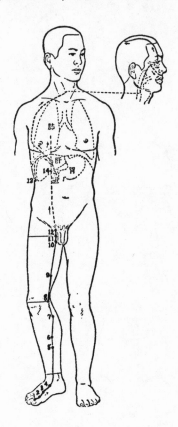

YIN 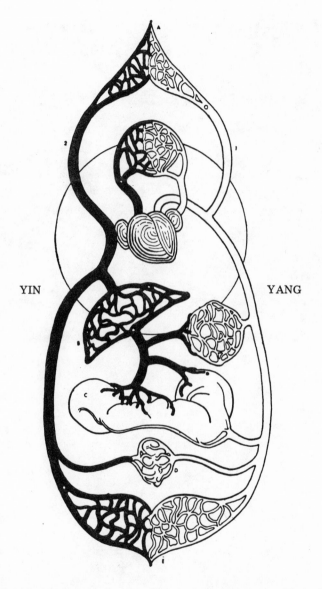 YANG

千古帝王之冠

考初民生活皆始於漁獵，次及游牧，繼以耕稼，居室火食衣服，自穴居生食卉服進化而來，社會之由草昧日進於開明，實多賴聖人之制作；且耕稼養人之效果極鉅，故民多樂從。

這時神農又以養人之道未周徧，因嘗百草之酸澀，察水泉之甘苦，令民知所取捨，從此，他神而化之，使民宜之，於是人民得居安食力，壽命得以延長，而養民之方日備。

CHAPTER FIVE
HERBS

Some of my friends have suggested this chapter on herbs. Although many medicines, such as ginseng are not available to the majority of people because of limited quantities and high costs, I have included a number of herbs and plants which are relatively accessible in markets and can even be grown or picked wild. Most beneficial herbs can be used as foods with common meals and can be properly included in one's diet for maximum benefit to health and vitality. Such herb preparations are tasty as well as useful in the prevention and cure of disorders and diseases.

When I first studied meditation under Master Kao, he advised me, first, to study the *I Ching,* which is the very source of meditation and a perfect guide to spirituality and enlightenment. Secondly, he advised me to know about acupuncture and herb medicine. Just as a traveler in a city should know the traffic, a person going into meditation should know what is actually happening inside his body, especially the directions of the breath and psychic energy *(ch'i).* Otherwise he is likely to get little or no benefit from meditation and may even have a reverse result.

Herbs can be instrumental in keeping the physiological balance of the metabolism or in restoring the balance when lost. Many ancient Taoists were also adept herbalists. Herbs were not only known to be beneficial to health but were believed to be, in a way, complementary to meditation. Meditation is an inner elixir, activating elements already existent in the body; herbs are an outer elixir, providing supplementary material for the same purpose.

GINSENG

The botanical name of ginseng is *Panax quinquefolium* or *Panax schinseng*. *Gin* means "person," and *seng* means "containing much nourishment." The root is of primary use as a medical preparation. Ginseng is a very slow-growing root which thrives only under specific conditions, requiring a cool, shady climate, like the shady side of a mountain. Ginseng can be prepared in many ways: with sugar, with wine, as a powder. It is especially good with chicken and in soups. Ginseng grows best in China, Korea, and Japan but it also grows wild in North America. The wild ginseng is the most desirable, particularly if the root lives to be many years old. There have been times when small quantities of wild ginseng have been bought and sold for great quantities of money.

Ginseng has the capacity to increase the vitality of the human body. It can cure certain illnesses, nourishing various organs of the body. It is considered a rejuvenator. It calms the mind and spirit. It makes the eyes shine brighter, increases happiness and wisdom. If it is taken regularly for long periods, it will make the body feel light and add to longevity. It can cure stomachaches and nausea and clears the blood of impurities. It is used mainly to increase the generative force of the human body. Modern scientific analysis has shown ginseng to contain phosphorus, potassium, calcium, magnesium, sodium, iron, aluminum, silicon, barium, strontium, manganese, titanium, glucose, and other elements.[1]

There is a Chinese legend abut ginseng, which was formerly produced in San-shi province on Tzu Tuan Shan ("Purple Round Mountain"). It is said that they had very old, divine ginseng there, the king and queen of all ginseng.

[1] Palos, Stephan, *The Chinese Art of Healing* (New York: Bantam Books, 1972), pp. 194-195.

It is said that a famous Taoist master built a monastery on the mountain there. Each day, he sent a disciple to the river to obtain water for their daily use. One day, while carrying water back to the monastery, the disciple encountered two young children, a boy and a girl, who asked for a drink from his jugs. After they had their drink, they disappeared.

When the disciple reached the monastery with two half-filled jugs, his master was angry with him. "Why are you so lazy?" he demanded. The disciple told the master about the young children, but because of the coldness and steepness of the mountains and the desolation of the area, the master was suspicious. He gave his disciple a ball of string, saying, "The next time the children ask for a drink from your jugs, tie this to them and we will follow them."

The next day, the disciple encountered the children and followed his master's instructions, tying the string to the boy's leg. The master and his disciple followed the string, and at its end found that it penetrated the ground among the rocks on a steep mountainside. They dug it up carefully, and found a large ginseng root, over a foot and a half tall. It had legs, hands, toes, fingers, and a head like a human being. On the head were a mouth, ears, and eyes half-open. They took the ginseng root back to the monastery and prepared it for cooking.

While the root was cooking, a messenger arrived with a request from a very high government official to meet immediately with the master. A coach was waiting to take him to the city. The master instructed his disciple to watch the ginseng carefully, but not to eat it. The disciple found the aroma so fragrant, that he could not resist taking first a small bite, and then more and more, until he had consumed the whole root. The disciple became immortal by doing this. Afterwards he grew afraid of the punishment he would receive when his master returned. He decided to run away, and to take a donkey with him. He gave some of the water from the pot of ginseng to the donkey. The donkey became immortal also. The disciple splashed the remainder of the water from the pot on the ground. The water suddenly grew into a cloud. The disciple and the donkey flew into the sky on this cloud.

It is said that the female ginseng grew so sad at the loss of her mate that she fearfully fled to the northeast of China. All the smaller ginseng followed her. Since then the Shangdang district no longer produces any ginseng.

One of China's eight spiritual immortals, Chang-Kuo, can be seen in ancient history books riding a donkey. He lived in the Chung Tiao Mountains near the place of the legend. During the T'ang dynasty Emperor Shuan-Tzung (713-755 A.D.) invited him to his court and honored him like a high official. The people of this area believe it was he who was the disciple of the Taoist master.

GARLIC

Garlic can be bought almost anywhere and is used as a seasoning with many dishes. The medicinal properties of garlic have been known for centuries. Its botanical name is *Allium sativum*. The stems, leaves, and root can be used. The taste of garlic is hot, and it has a strong odor. The root is a round bulb. It can be used in frying or cooking with other foods, or it can be eaten raw. The root is used in herbal preparations. It generates warmth in the body.

Garlic is used in treating ulcers, colds, tuberculosis, digestive disorders, rheumatism, loss of appetite, pimples, and excess phlegm. It stimulates the generative force, is an antidote for various poisons and is used to clean drinking water of pollutants. Garlic can be prepared as a drink, applied externally as an ointment combined with mugwort, or used as a poultice.

A friend of mine, who is a vegetarian, eats garlic cloves like chewing gum. He is ninety-five years old.

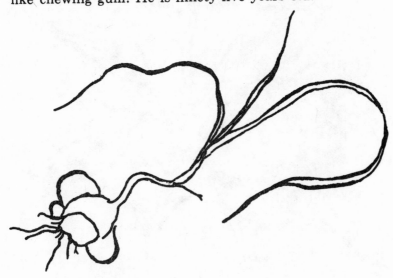

TANGERINE

The botanical name of the tangerine is *Aurantii cortex*. It is grown predominantly in the southern part of China. The best variety is found in Canton province. The peel is the part which is primarily used. Its taste is somewhat bitter. It is thin, unlike the skin of the orange. It can be used fresh or dried. It is used in the treatment of excessive belching, urinary disorders, indigestion, bladder inflammations, intestinal disorders, cholera, body odors, and coughing and as an aid in spiritual development. It can be taken as a tea or combined with other herbs.

GINGER

The botanical name for ginger is *Zingiber officinale*. Ginger has a hot taste and is high in calories. It is used in cooking and as an herb preparation. It is primarily the root that is used, both fresh and dried. For herbal uses it is best when dried. In cooking it can be used with fish and meat.

Ginger is useful in treating colds, stomach disorders, distended stomach, rheumatism excess phlegm, and fever. It helps in producing sweat, aids appetite and digestion, and relieves headaches and excessive belching. In China ginger is used by doctors as a medication. If it is eaten regularly it will help make the mind and spirit clear. Confucius used it daily: "He was never without ginger when he ate."[2]

[2] Legge, James, ed., *The Chinese Classics* (Hong Kong: Hong Kong University Press, 1960), Vol. 1, p. 233.

HO SHOU WU

Next to ginseng, Ho Shou Wu *(Polygonatum multifolium)* is the most popular medical herb in China. It is a relatively new discovery, the earliest authentic record in medical books being A.D. 806.

As in the case of ginseng, it is the root which contains its most potent properties; the older the root, the more effective it is. According to traditional medicine, it can control or cure a variety of ailments, including cardiovascular ones. It is also believed to prevent or cure anemia and restore the color of graying hair. But—again like ginseng—it is its capacity to increase generative force that gives the plant its tremendous reputation.

Ho Shou Wu, the legend goes, was a man who lived in Honan province. He was physically weak and sexually impotent, and at fifty-eight was still unmarried. One day, lying down in the fields, he saw a vine whose branches were intertwined in a spontaneous embrace. Ho Shou Wu dug out its potato-like root, went home, cooked it, and ate it. Immediately he felt a new vitality and sexual capacity. To the surprise of his father, who didn't believe his story, Ho Shou Wu soon married, had three sons, and lived to be 160 years old.

HWANG CHING

Hwang Ching *(Polygonatum giganteum* var. *Thunbergii),* which grows in many mountains and valleys of China, is recorded in medical books and has a variety of functions. It increases vitality, cures rheumatism, and benefits inner organs. It is also believed to make the body feel light, even weightless.

A maid servant, having made some domestic mistake, ran to the mountains to escape her master's punishment. With nothing to eat, she spotted an herb and ate it on the spot without cooking it. She felt light in body and could soon fly in the air. When the master heard of this he became afraid that the maid, with her newly acquired capacity, might retaliate his harsh treatment of her and do him harm. He consulted a sage who attributed the maid's new vitality to the ingestion of hwang ching. He advised the master to arrange for a mountain feast in such a way that the maid would partake of food, which would cause her to regain her weight and stop levitating.

LOTUS

Lotus grows in the water. It has large round leaves and long stems, like an umbrella. The flower is red, pink, and white. In Chinese poetry, beautiful women are often compared to lotus blossoms. The lotus flowers in July and August. The leaves, seeds, and root can be cooked. The leaves and root are used in herbal preparations. The leaves help to diminish thirst and expel poisons. The lotus is widely used in women's disorders. The part of the leaf near the stem connection, called the "nose of the lotus," helps in pregnancy to make the fetus firm in the uterus. The leaf is used to make soap.

The lotus flower can be eaten with sugar. It helps cure dysentery and diarrhea. In the autumn, as the lotus sinks, it is collected, dried and made into a powder. The seeds are used to calm the heart. If eaten regularly, lotus increases vitality, rejuvenates, and makes the body light. The root, which grows under water, is eaten cooked or raw, and is used as a powder for many foods. As an herbal preparation it is used for cholera, calming the spirit, reducing thirst, and aiding appetite and digestion. It makes a person look and feel younger and increases longevity.

MUSTARD

The botanical names of mustard are *Sinapis nigra* and *Sinapis alba*. The mustard seeds are the part of the plant used. Mustard has a hot taste and a strong odor. It is used in the cure of kidney, ear, eye, and nose disorders. If it is eaten regularly it provides warmth to the body as well as calories. There are two varieties of mustard, black and white. The white is most common in the East, the black in the West. Mustard is used in curing colds, intestinal disorders, childhood fevers, and headache. It can be used as a poultice over an inflamed area. If applied to the skin one can feel heat immediately. Western doctors refine it into an oil, which is very strong and should be mixed with wheat flour, or it will burn the skin.

MUGWORT

The botanical name of mugwort is *Artemesia vulgaris*.
Mugwort is widely used in China in moxa treatment in
acupuncture. Boiled as a drink it aids in curing dysentery,
diarrhea, and the coughing of blood. It is a vitalizer, and
prevents colds and rheumatism. It aids in pregnancy.

YARROW

The botanical name of yarrow is *Achillea millefolium*. The yarrow stalk is familiar from its use in casting the *I Ching* oracle. The root is used as an herb. It has a slight sweet taste and a warm character. It aids in curing piles, ulcers, carbuncles, skin wounds that have opened, and overall weakness.

CLAMS AND OYSTERS

Clams are found widely along the coast of China. They are cultivated as well. Both the clam itself and the shell are useful in treating disorders. The shell is boiled in water or vinegar and the solution is used to treat ulcers, boils, and gastric disorders.

Oysters thrive among the rocks and pools of the seashore. The shell is used in treatment of vomiting, fever, coughing, asthma, and lung disorders.

ALMONDS

The botanical name for the almond is *Prunus amygdalus.*
There are two kinds of almonds, one sweet, the other
bitter. The bitter almond is slightly poisonous, and this
element must be removed. The oil of bitter almond is
helpful in curing fevers and headaches. The oil of sweet
almond is used in treating coughs, throat irritations, and
stomach and intestinal disorders. Almond is also used in
cooking.

TORTOISE

The tortoise, or turtle, both lake and ocean varieties, can be eaten for its fine meat. If eaten reglarly, it increases vitality and makes the body feel light. Tortoise shell is used for both divination and medicinal purposes. It helps to cure intestinal disorders, piles, malaria, skin sores, boils, scalp disease, fever, stomach ache, backache, and pains of the limbs.

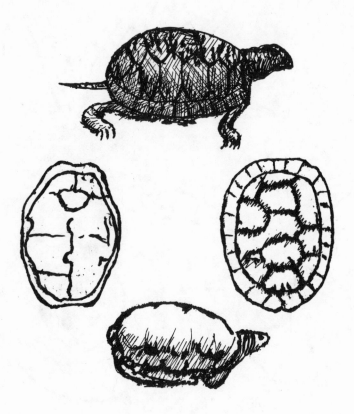

道家養生術

（註八）之意。清雍
正十一年，動支國
帑，恢廓基址，構
造陵廟，如附圖。
（註九）

神農之遠遊，
殆如淮南子所說，
「欲嘗百草之滋味
，水泉之甘苦，令
民知所避就，」可
謂勞苦極了！

上古之時，江
漢之區，皆爲黎境
。黎卽犂，乃農具
之名。黎民卽耕稼
之民。按犂之義爲
利，利於發土壤，絕草根。犂從牛，乃用牛耕田之意。（見附圖）
蚩尤爲九黎之君，乃炎族之支派，初爲黃帝勁敵，卒爲黃帝所敗。

神農嘗百草圖（採自三才圖會）（註七）

CHAPTER SIX
FOODS

Ko Hung, a famous Taoist and medical doctor, wrote in his book *Po Pu Tze*:

> Use medicine and food to nourish the body, and technique (massage and exercise) to prolong the life.

Certainly the knowledge of eating and drinking properly is very important to maintaining health and increasing longevity. This is a fact that has long been recognized by Taoists. The *I Ching* says "the superior man is careful in his words, and temperate in eating and drinking." Therefore, as the old Chinese saying warns, "Disaster comes from the mouth, sickness comes in through the mouth."

Food and herbs are closely related. Foods contain protein, fats, and carbohydrates as well as herbal properties such as vitamins, minerals, and other health-giving elements. Likewise, poor nutrition is a primary cause of sickness. Just as a person who doesn't eat for a day may feel uncomfortable, tired, and weak, and if he continues his fast may even die, a person who eats improperly over a long period of time will become weaker, more susceptible to illness, and may very well shorten his life.

Confucius wrote about food in several of his books. In the *Chung Yung* (Doctrine of the Mean), he says: "Everybody drinks and eats, but few can distinguish the flavors." He doesn't mean that people cannot distinguish one food from another, but that they are unaware of the connection between flavors and health. In the *Shu Ching,* he describes the relationship of the five flavors to the five elements and to the five human organs.

In the book of medical science, the *Nei Ching*, written after Confucius, the importance of maintaining a balance between the five flavors was further explained.

Recently Chinese medical doctors have analyzed this information in light of current medical knowledge as follows:

Sour This taste is related to the wood element. It strengthens the liver and operates against the stomach. It is the flavor that stimulates the appetite and can be used to preserve food as in pickling. Vinegar, lemon, and certain plums are sources of the sour taste. If one eats too much sour food, however, it discolors and decays the teeth and injures the stomach and intestines. In the northwest part of China, in San Shih and Shen Shih, the people are fond of the sour taste.

Sweet This flavor belongs to the earth element and is most concentrated in honey and sugar. It is also found in fruits and certain grains. This is a very popular taste as sweetness is the main quality of candy, cookies, and desserts. If there were no sugar, many businesses would close and children would be very unhappy. The sweet flavor helps digestion, makes the skin smooth, and keeps the stomach and intestines moist and in good repair. Overeating sweet food, however, will weaken the heart, hurt the omentum, cause diabetes, and result in weight gain.

Bitter Of the five flavors, the bitter taste is related to fire. Its function is to strengthen the heart, and its quality is cold. It makes the eyes clear and bright and reduces mental anxiety. Among vegetables the bitter taste is found in escarole and in Chinese bitter melon, which people eat in the summer. It is not a popular taste in food, but is often a quality of medicine. A common Chinese saying is: "The good medicine is bitter, but it cures the disease." Old people should not take too much bitter flavor as it will make them weak.

Spicy The spicy or hot flavor belongs to the metal element and comes from ginger, garlic, onions, and red and black pepper. It is beneficial to the lungs, and can cure colds and rheumatism. Spicy flavors increase the appetite, help digestion, and stimulate perspiration, but an excess can injure the stomach and liver and create or aggravate hemorrhoids. These flavors are popular in the mountainous provinces of Hunan and Szechuan in southwest China because the winds there make it easy to catch cold. Now restaurants specializing in Hunan and Szechuan cuisine are becoming very popular in America, as well as East Indian restaurants which also serve hot and spicy food.

Salt This flavor is related to the water element since salt comes from the sea. It is widely used in food and has many medicinal and other uses. It aids in the function of the kidneys, helps digestion, reduces fever, diminishes poisonous substances, and generally strengthens the body. If there is no salt in the diet the body will become weak. It is indispensable in cooking for "If there is no salt, there is no taste." But if there is an excess, high blood pressure and heart attacks can result. Salt is often used to preserve vegetables and meat just as it was in ancient times. It can also be used as a tooth powder, or dissolved in water and used as a mouthwash, an eyewash, or to rinse the nostrils and keep the nasal passages clear. Tired feet and legs will feel better after soaking in a salt solution. Drinking salt water in the evening and morning is used in China to prevent constipation.

In short, each of the five flavors should be used, but in moderation. In this way we can gain maximum benefits from each flavor and avoid the harm that results from excess.

GRAINS

Even though Confucius was an aristocrat and knew the tastes of expensive foods, he also knew about the less expensive foods which were good for health. In the *Analects*, he writes:

> The Master said, "With coarse rice to eat, with water to drink, and my bended arm for a pillow, I have still joy in the midst of these things."

Confucius knew that this simple food could nourish the body and prevent sickness. He knew that the people could not even think of joy if they were always sick. Now, 2,500 years later, we are just beginning to realize that brown rice is more nutritious than white rice. Not only does it contain more of the B vitamins, but it has a greater fiber content as well.

In addition to the brown and white varieties, there is a shorter, stickier type called glutinous or pearl rice which supplies a high level of energy. It can either be cooked or made into flour. The flour is an ingredient for many Chinese foods and candies. However, it is sticky and difficult to digest and therefore is not good for old or sick people.

Wheat is also an important food in China and in the West. It is used to make bread, noodles, and dumplings. Wheat contains protein, carbohydrates, and a number of important vitamins. Wheat sprouts can be used to make sugar, and can be dried to make medicines. Dried wheat sprouts are helpful in treating indigestion.

Sesame is another food with a high nutritional value and many uses. White sesame makes the skin smooth and moist and black sesame is good for the hair. They are especially effective when combined with other foods. Both sesame oil and sesame paste are delicious ingredients in many dishes. The oil may be used medicinally to diminish poisons.

Like the other grains, corn contains protein and carbohydrates but is an especially good source of sugar. It can be eaten fresh or ground into meal or flour. Corn makes a fine oil which is effective in the treatment of difficulties in urinating.

The oil is also good for the heart. Chinese doctors use the silk as a medicine for diabetes.

Pearl barley is a highly nutritious grain which is easy to digest. Recent research by the Japanese experts indicates that it contains 17 percent protein, which is significantly higher than other grains. It also contains 7 percent oil and is rich in phosphorus. Pearl barley has been used by Chinese and Japanese medical doctors as an indispensable element in cancer therapy. It is also effective in reducing swelling due to water retention and eases the pain of rheumatism. In addition to its medicinal uses, pearl barley is highly nutritious, so several times a week I prepare it with brown rice and various beans.

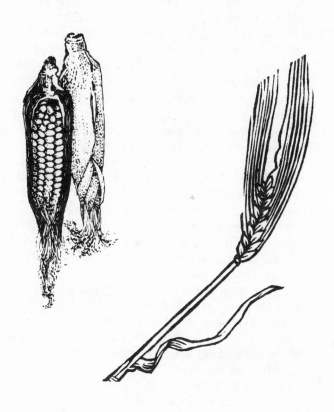

BEANS

Beans are an excellent food. In fact, beans are more nutritious than either brown rice or wheat. There are numerous kinds of beans—round, long, kidney-shaped—and they come in a variety of colors. All beans are high in quality protein, calories (energy), and vitamins B_1 and B_2. Beans can be processed to make many different kinds of food. Soybeans are the most versatile. Food, oil, fiber for clothing, and other industrial products are all made from soybeans. Among the foods derived from soybeans in both the East and West are soy sauce, tofu, and soybean paste (which the Japanese call miso).

Tofu is an especially healthful food. Discovered in 120 B.C., it is considered by many doctors to be better than meat because although it has a high protein content, it contains no cholesterol, saturated fats, or poisons. Tofu is also easy to digest, nonfattening, and can prevent disease.

Beans can also be soaked and fried or boiled. The whole bean can then be eaten alone or with meat or vegetables. Prepared this way, beans retain all their nutritional value, but older people may have trouble digesting them. An alternative method is to soak the beans, then mash them and combine them with eggs and perhaps some vegetables and fry. This makes a wonderful meal in which all the nutritional value of the beans is retained and it is easily digested.

Additionally, most beans can be sprouted. Bean sprouts are tender, delicious, and because of their life spirit, highly nutritious. Beans can also be ground to make flour from which many foods can be prepared.

In China there are many kinds of beans and they are related by their colors to the five elements:

1. *Yellow*: The soybean is yellow and therefore in theory, is related to the earth element. Soybeans benefit the stomach and spleen and are used to make soy sauce and tofu.
2. *Red*: Red beans are of the fire element and are good for the heart and beneficial to the blood. They strengthen the spleen, facilitate weight loss, increase the flow of urine, diminish swelling, and improve conditions such as rheuma-

tism. Street peddlers in Taiwan and Japan make a special soup and cold drink from sweetened red beans. They are inexpensive, tasty, and good for health.

3. *Black*: The black bean is related to the water element and therefore benefits the kidneys. Black beans make the skin smooth, the eyes bright, and the heart calm. Black beans also repair tissue, diminish poisons and swelling in the foot or leg, facilitate urination, improve rheumatism, and increase sexual energy.

4. *Green*: Mung beans are green and belong to the wood element. Their quality is cold and therefore can reduce fevers and diminish poisons. In the summer a soup can be prepared of mung beans and kombu (seaweed), which is called "Blue dragon goes to the green sea." It is used for fevers and to eliminate poisons and is also helpful for acne, but it is too cold for the aged and weak, who should eat only small portions. In China, a sweet drink is made from mung beans and peppermint and is sold in coffee shops and by street peddlers.

5. *White*: White beans belong to the metal element and benefit the lungs. They are shaped like kidneys and therefore also benefit the kidneys. They are more starchy than other beans and can be fried, mashed and sweetened to make a delightful sweet paste.

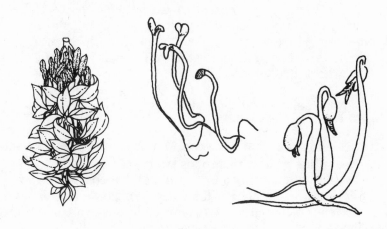

VEGETABLES

Vegetables are highly nutritious foods rich in important vitamins and minerals. In the last few years, more and more people have stopped eating meat and become vegetarians. Ancient Taoists believed in eating everything, including meat, in moderation. However, meat is becoming a more dangerous food because it contains greater concentrations of pesticides than vegetables since animals are higher in the food chain. Also, farmers inject their animals with hormones and other drugs that remain in their bodies after they are killed. Vegetarians, doctors are finding, have lower incidences of high blood pressure, heart problems, cancer, and arthritis.

Some doctors are recommending a vegetarian diet for cancer patients. For instance, my friend Dr. William Chao is an expert in treating cancer with Chinese herbs and diet. He has found that fish are especially dangerous for people with malignancies. One of my students visited Dr. Chao several years ago when a cancerous tumor was discovered in his chest. Dr. Chao treated him with herbs and a vegetarian diet. His tumor disappeared and there was no need for an operation. Today he is in very good health.

Meat is still an important food for some people because of its high protein content. In fact, for elderly people or those who are recovering from illnesses or operations, meat is a more effective food than vegetables. This was known by Mencius, who said:

> When people reach sixty years old, if they have no meat they cannot be well nourished.

Of course, in 300 B.C., when Mencius lived, there was no tofu or other protein-rich foods available.

In any event, eating a balanced diet that contains a variety of fruits and vegetables will help avoid many serious diseases.

Listed are several important vegetables which contain different nutritional and medicinal values.

142

Celery It is highly nutritious and contains vitamins A, B and C and the mineral elements potassium and sodium. It looks good—fresh and green like jade. Because of its color it is beneficial to the heart and is used medicinally to cure high blood pressure and rheumatism. Eating celery can help reduce weight as well. It can be fried or blanched in boiling water. It should always be cooked quickly to preserve its vitamins and minerals. Celery is very fibrous and some people, especially the elderly and sick, find it difficult to chew. Therefore it makes a good juice either alone or in combination with other vegetables such as carrots and radishes. To make the juice even more tasty, fruits can be added.

Spinach This vegetable contains large amounts of vitamin B and iron. It is green, tender, and tastes good as well as having excellent nutritional and medical value. Many Western doctors now suggest eating more greens to benefit the heart. Chinese doctors have advised this for centuries because green relates to the wood element which is vital to the heart. Spinach is one of the greenest vegetables. It should be fried quickly or cooked in boiling water for a minute or two to avoid destroying its beneficial elements. It can accompany other vegetables or be cooked with a meal of bean curd, tomatoes and eggs. Such a meal is delicious, nutritious, and attractive. If we add black wood ear mushrooms to this meal it would contain all the five colors—white, green, red, yellow, and black—which represent the five elements. Such a meal is characteristic of Chinese cooking, which should always be colorful, tasty, and aromatic.

Cabbage This is an inexpensive vegetable which contains vitamin B and sugar. It is easy to digest and can be cooked in the same manner as celery or spinach and seasoned with soy sauce and sesame oil. It can also be cut in pieces and seasoned with salt, ginger, and red pepper. After one or two days add sesame oil. Prepared in this way it is very delicious and still contains all its nutritional elements. Some Chinese restaurants serve it as a complementary salad to regular customers.

Radish This vegetable contains various vitamins. Radishes come in white, red, and green and are either round or long. They may be cooked like other vegetables or eaten raw. In China a radish is grown which is both green outside and inside. It has the consistency of a pear and is eaten like a fruit because it is juicy and not hot. It is used to reduce fever and is especially beneficial to people who heat their homes with charcoal or coal in the winter because it reduces the effect of the poisons released into the air by burning these materials. For people who eat meat, raw radishes make the mouth feel cleaner as they cut through fat. Medicinally, radishes can cure fever and the pain of sore throat. For more serious cases, especially in the spring, radishes may be combined with olives and eaten raw. or cooked together in boiling water. The leaves of the radish should not be neglected as they are even more powerful in their medicinal properties than the root. They are tasty when fried with other vegetables.

Carrot Everyone knows of the high nutritional value of this vegetable which contains sugar, protein, and vitamins A and B among others. It also contains carotene, which has recently been shown to decrease the incidence of lung cancer and may be beneficial in the prevention of other cancers as well. Carrots increase red blood cells and the redder the carrot, the better it is. It can be cut into small, thin pieces and cooked with Chinese fine noodles and peanuts. This dish is served as a special food by many families at the Chinese New Year. If the teeth are strong, carrots can be cleaned and eaten raw. Not only will they retain all their beneficial elements, but they will also strengthen the teeth. Older people whose teeth are not strong or who suffer indigestion from eating carrots should drink carrot juice either alone or combined with other vegetable juices.

Onion This vegetable has a very high nutritional value and is also a useful treatment for colds and fevers. It strengthens the body like garlic, but it has a very hot taste and leaves a bad odor in the mouth. It can be fried alone or with other vegetables, eggs, or meat. But it is most effective when eaten raw. Some people place slices on a sandwich of cheese and tomato.

Tomato This is a very attractive vegetable, red in color and round like a ball, either big or small. It contains vitamins B and C and can be cooked as a vegetable or eaten raw like a fruit. In combination with other vegetables in a salad or other dishes it provides wonderful color. It cannot, however, be cooked too much or it becomes sour. Combined with oxtail it makes a delicious and nutritious soup.

Red Pepper This is another vegetable with a hot taste. It is widely used in China, India, and Indonesia, but should be eaten in moderation because of its hot properties. Actually, it is very nutritious and includes some vitamins not found in other vegetables. Medicinally, it is used to make the eyes bright and increase heat in the body. A friend told me that if my feet were cold in the winter a small amount of powdered red pepper in my socks would make them warm. It did.

Cucumber This vegetable is easy to obtain and inexpensive. It is very good for nutrition and is mostly eaten raw in salads. Eating cucumbers makes the skin smooth and soft. Medicinally they can be used to reduce fever, but eating an excess of this vegetable will make the body weak because of its cold properties.

Watercress This vegetable is not found in China and therefore its name, *shih yang ts'ai*, means "Western vegetable." It is popular in the West as it has a high nutritional value and is readily available at a reasonable price. It can cure many diseases such as high blood pressure and fevers and makes the eyes bright. Because it is green it is also beneficial to the heart.

Green Onion Also known as "scallion," this is a hot vegetable which is available throughout the year. In China it grows in the winter and is yellowish-green and tastes sweet. In some places they grow very large and one onion may weigh half a pound. They contain many elements for strengthening sexual energy and are good in combination with meat, hard bean curd or other vegetables.

Potato The potato, both sweet and plain, and other root vegetables such as taro may be regarded as supplementary foods. They have both nutritional and medicinal value. The taro and the sweet potato, either boiled or dried, are effective against scrofulous lumps and swellings. The sweet potato is also beneficial to the skin and aids digestion. It is more nutritious than other root vegetables. In places where rice and/or other grains aren't grown, people eat sweet potato as the main food. Such people are generally healthy and live long lives. Research indicates that sweet potatoes leave less waste in the body than grains. The waste products of grains do not cause sickness but do accelerate the deterioration of the body. Thus, when a Taoist reaches a high level, he follows "Pi Ku," which means avoiding grains. His diet then consists of sweet potatoes, taro, dried fruits such as dates and walnuts, chestnuts and pine nuts.

Seaweed Besides the more usual vegetables a great variety of vegetables grow in the sea. The oceans produce as many different kinds of vegetables and animals as the land. In the future, it is likely that more of our food will come from the sea because the expanding human population will naturally learn to exploit the abundance that already grows there and only needs to be harvested. In the island countries of Taiwan and Japan, where the land area cannot produce enough food for the population, people have turned to the sea to supplement the food supply. Recently, the people of Taiwan have harvested many kinds of seaweeds and researched their uses as food and medicine. Many of these have been found to be edible and nutritious and are processed and packaged in cans. Furthermore, sea animals, fish, and shellfish are abundant in the oceans. Most are low in fats and cholesterol, but recently it has been discovered that they often contain poisons due to chemical waste and oil which has leaked into the sea and, therefore, may be dangerous to eat. Seaweeds, because they are at the bottom of the food chain, are not affected as much. There are thousands of kinds of seaweeds. We will mention just a few.

1. *Hai Tai*: The name of this sea vegetable means sea belt be-

cause of its long, narrow shape. Called *kombu* by the Japanese, it is green in color, inexpensive, and easily available. Cooking *hai tai* is easy as it only needs to be placed in warm water to soften it. This seaweed can be eaten alone or in combination with meat. *Hai tai* contains iron, iodine, calcium, and phosphorus and is valuable in the treatment of high blood pressure, problems of the cartilage of the windpipe, and hair loss. It can also improve the condition of hardened blood vessels. Pieces of the vegetable applied to burns and other skin problems such as pimples will help healing.

2. *Tzu Ts'ai*: This sea vegetable is called laver in English and is actually an edible marine algae. It is thinner than paper and harvested near the shores of China and Japan. Deep purple in color, it contains iron, iodine, calcium, and phosphorus. It is effective in the treatment of an enlarged thyroid gland. Colorful and delicious, *tzu ts'ai* can be cooked in soup with eggs or used to wrap rice. It should not, however, be overcooked. *Tzu ts'ai* is used to treat kidney problems and goiter.

FRUITS

Fruits contain many important dietary elements such as vitamins, minerals, and fruit sugar, and are necessary to supplement other foods and vegetables. However, not all countries have a favorable climate for producing fruits, and transportation systems were not always as developed as today. Therefore, many people are not in the habit of eating fruits. Chinese books of pharmacology list hundreds of fruits as medicines, and recently Western medical doctors have found that many nutrients are easily obtained from fruits. Because they can be eaten raw, no nutritional values are lost through cooking and no time is lost in preparation. Thus, fruits are a very important class of food. Certainly, a piece of fruit before a meal serves as a stimulant to the appetite, and afterwards, eating fruit for dessert helps digestion.

Fruits, like vegetables, have thousands of varieties. We will list several which are easy to obtain, inexpensive, not limited by seasons, and which have the most nutritional and medicinal value.

Banana This fruit is good for people of all ages as it is easy to chew and has a skin which keeps it fresh. It contains vitamins A and C as well as protein and fruit sugar. Medicinally, bananas are good for coughs, foot diseases, and hemorrhoids. They break down fat and aid digestion, especially after eating meat. Bananas also help relieve constipation. If it is a serious case, they can be used very effectively in combination with sesame oil. They are very good for the aged and sick, but, because they contain more calories than other fruit, they are not recommended for the overweight.

Orange Oranges and their cousins, tangerines, are sweet fruits high in vitamin C. They protect the circulatory system and strengthen the body against germs, thereby preventing colds and other infections. However, the most valuable part of the fruit for medicinal purposes is the peel and the stringy membrane inside, which most people throw away. The peel helps digestion and stops coughs. It is an important material in Chinese herbal therapy and is also good for cooking. Marmalade, made from all parts of the orange including the peel, is very popular.

Grapefruit The grapefruit has similar food value as other members of the citrus family. Some are very big, others are smaller, and all contain large amounts of vitamin C. The taste is a bit sour. Grapefruit neutralizes sugar and fat and aids in weight loss. Medicinally the grapefruit promotes a clear mind, calms the circulation, and is beneficial to the heart and the digestive process. It can diminish phlegm, reduce mouth odors, cure fevers of the stomach and lungs, and relieve constipation. The dried peel can be a valuable medicine. Boiled in water it relieves indigestion and is also indispensable in cooking. It imparts a pleasing flavor to meat and increases both nutritional and medicinal values of food.

Apple The nutritional value of the apple is known in both the East and the West. Apples contain vitamin C, iron, and calcium. They are beneficial for the stomach and intestines and aid the digestive process. They also clean poisons from the body and are an effective cure for headaches, insomnia, dysentery, and diarrhea. One apple after a meal has great benefits for health. And, as the saying goes, "An apple a day keeps the doctor away."

Papaya This fruit contains large amounts of vitamin C and sugar. It can be cooked or eaten raw when mature. Medicinally it is effective against inflamed gums, blood poisoning, and bleeding in the tissue. When cooked together with the seeds from inside plum pits it effectively combats lung disease and coughing.

Pear Pears are available all year long but are especially good in the autumn. At this time of the year the weather suddenly changes from hot and dry to cool and damp, and people are more prone to get sick. Eating a pear each day can prevent many diseases. Pears contain vitamin A, are sweet, and their quality is cold. They diminish fevers of the stomach and intestine, reduce thirst, cure coughs, reduce phlegm, and even help people who have suffered strokes. A slice of pear may also be applied to burns or other skin problems. While pears are often eaten raw, the aged and sick should eat them cooked. There are many ways to prepare them. They can be boiled or steamed with honey or sugar. Or, juice extracted from cooked pears can be made into a thick syrup by adding sugar or honey. One spoonful of this syrup added to water makes a delightful drink.

Olive There are several kinds of olives, both big and small. They contain more iron than other fruits and can be eaten raw or prepared with salt, as in China, or in brine, as in the West. They are used to cure a dry mouth, chapped lips, and a swollen tongue. They are also effective when the face is flushed and hot and the ears are hot or ringing. Also, eating olives will soften and diminish a fishbone that is caught in the throat.

Watermelon This is a favorite fruit in the summer. It is very sweet and juicy and contains sugar, fat, and protein. Watermelon can prevent heat stroke, lower high blood pressure, help digestion, aid kidney problems, relieve constipation, and increase the flow of urine. However, it is very cold and eating too much may make the legs and waist painful. The seeds can be removed from the pits and made into candy, and the rind, when prepared with either salt and sugar or sugar alone, is effective in reducing fevers.

Persimmon There are various kinds of persimmons. Some are yellow and others are red like tomatoes. They contain vitamin A, and are cold in quality. When fresh and soft they are very sweet but when hard they will make the mouth pucker. They can be preserved by drying, making them available all year long. Persimmons stimulate the appetite. They are very good when steamed. The powder which forms on the outside of the dried fruit helps hemorrhoids. Persimmon boiled in water is an effective treatment for colds and fevers and relieves bodily discomfort.

Lemon This is a very important fruit but is rarely eaten alone because of its sour taste. It is most often used in food as flavoring. Lemon contains vitamins A and C and is medicinally used to prevent fatigue, strengthen the blood vessels, and prevent the skin from aging. In China it is used to cook chicken and other meats, making them tender and tasty.

CHAPTER SEVEN
PATTING THE EIGHT PSYCHIC CHANNELS

Chen T'wan, a famous Taoist philosopher of the tenth century, is the legendary creator of a health and relaxation technique called Patting the Eight Psychic Channels. This exercise is related to both acupuncture and massage, but differs in the method used to restore balance to the body. By stimulating the Eight Psychic Channels with vigorous patting using this ancient technique, the muscles, bones, and nervous system are benefited.

In China this is a very popular treatment that is commonly taken in a barbershop or public bath. Most of the natural hot springs in Taiwan offer this service, usually rendered by blind men. Patting is also performed in the home by practitioners who walk the street calling out *"sung ku,"* which means "relax the bone." Other practitioners can be reached by telephone or through an agent to arrange a home treatment.

Patting the Eight Psychic Channels is also used by adepts in several of the martial arts, including inner schools such as T'ai Chi and outer schools such as Shao Lin. Hands and sticks are used in the initial stages of training while the force of the patting is gradually increased. At the highest levels, the practitioner uses hammers or bricks. In Shao Lin the exercise is performed with a knife or hammer with great force. This helps the practitioner harden his muscles and bones, as well as stimulating the psychic channels to improve health and strength. The use of any object other than the hands is not recommended until the highest levels of achievement have been reached in the martial arts.

The Eight Psychic Channels which were discussed and illustrated in Chapter Four are the pathways of sexual energy. People who are old or sick are often deficient in this energy. Their channels become blocked and little or no energy can penetrate the body. This is especially true for people past

THE PSYCHIC CENTERS

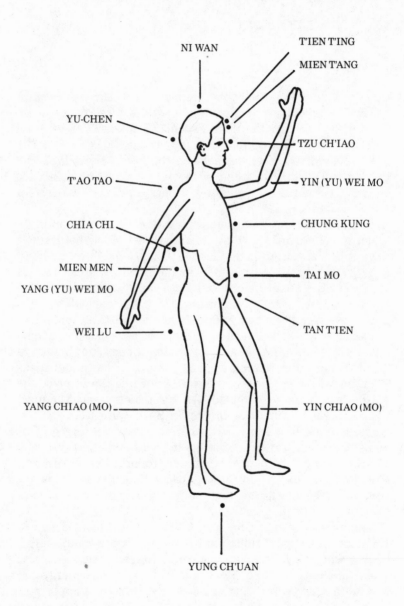

NI WAN

T'IEN T'ING

MIEN T'ANG

YU-CHEN

TZU CH'IAO

T'AO TAO

YIN (YU) WEI MO

CHIA CHI

CHUNG KUNG

MIEN MEN

YANG (YU) WEI MO

TAI MO

WEI LU

TAN T'IEN

YANG CHIAO (MO)

YIN CHIAO (MO)

YUNG CH'UAN

middle age. Their bodies, like machines that have not been maintained properly, refuse to function. For example, a car whose gas line is blocked cannot deliver any fuel to the engine; consequently the engine is unable to perform its function of moving the car. The problem is to find and remove the cause of stagnation and thus repair the condition. It is similar for human beings.

There are several ways to stimulate all the psychic channels with patting. Sometimes the entire channel may be patted. In other cases it may be best to pat only a portion of the channel. Often it is only necessary to pat one of the many psychic centers located on the channel. Psychic centers are important points where *ch'i* is stored. Patting releases this energy, helping to propel the flow of *ch'i* through the psychic channel, just as removing a dam will release a powerful flood of water that will remove any areas of stagnation in the river.

To use this technique, first find which psychic channels relate to the person's health problem and then treat these channels by patting the appropriate psychic centers. This will stimulate the inner organs, make both the *ch'i* and the blood flow more freely, thus restoring the body to its normal healthy condition, like that of a young person.

Patting can be done at any time and in any place. You may find that some areas of the body require greater attention while others need little. While the palms are commonly used for patting, the fist may be used in a variety of ways. When closed loosely, as if holding peanuts, the fist provides three surfaces for patting: the flat part of the fingers between the knuckles, and both the small finger and thumb sides of the fist. With an imaginary walnut in the hand, the knuckles become the patting surface. In addition to using the palm or fist, one may use the edge of the outstretched hand. For patting the joints, curl the hands and use just the fingertips. Finally, this exercise should be avoided by pregnant women, people who have recently suffered a heart attack or stroke, and those with conditions such as diabetes, tuberculosis, high blood pressure, kidney disorders, metastatic cancer, or inflamed joints.

TAN T'IEN

The *Tan T'ien* is the most important psychic center in the Taoist system and is located between the navel and the pubic bone. Its name means "the place which produces elixir" and refers to the process by which the stomach transforms food into blood, which is then transformed into sexual energy and finally becomes *ch'i*. It is both the meeting place for many of the psychic channels (see pages 96-98), and the body's center of gravity. In addition to the production and storage of blood and ova or sperm, this area also processes the body's waste and prepares it for elimination. When this part of the body malfunctions, such problems as indigestion, infections, constipation, and various types of cancer manifest themselves. Therefore, it is important to eat the proper foods and use patting to make this vital center work effectively.

Psychic Patting of the *Tan T'ien* should cover the whole region from the navel to the pubic bone thereby including other important points such as *Ch'i Hai* (Sea of Breath). Use the hands, starting very lightly, and pat the *Tan T'ien* forty-eight times with your open hand. While forty-eight is the standard number, you can do more or less depending on the amount of time you have available. This helps blood circulation as well as the circulation of *ch'i*. It also aids intestinal function, preventing constipation and other abdominal problems. Women with menstrual difficulties can also gain relief by patting this center.

WEI LU

The second psychic center is called *Wei Lu*, the Gate of the Tail. It is located in the gluteal region (buttocks). Because of the preponderance of ligaments, sinews, and bones in this area, it is sometimes difficult for the *ch'i* to enter the channel of control or the spinal cord. Therefore, we use patting to loosen the area, facilitating the flow of *ch'i*. This is beneficial for general health, especially for the prevention and cure of lower back problems, as well as being essential to the practice of meditation.

Use the back of hands, fingers slightly closed, for the upper buttocks (gluteus medius) and the thumb side of the hands, fingers closed, for the lower (gluteus maximus). Pat forty-eight times. For health purposes, special attention should be given to the area at the top of the hipbones, the iliac crest. This area is often tight or tense, especially in people with sedentary life-styles. Pat with the sides of the fists an additional forty-eight times.

MIEN MEN

The third psychic center is called *Mien Men*, the Gate of Life, in the lower back and waist. Both the kidneys and adrenal glands are connected with this center. The kidneys are responsible for blood purification and hormone production. The adrenals also produce various hormones and regulate such functions as maintenance of body temperature and blood pressure. In addition, they play an important role in the body's ability to deal with stress from both internal and external sources and, through hormone production, affect the utilization and storage of fats and sugar.

Patting this area, using either the side or back of the fist, can help prevent and cure disorders related to kidney and adrenal function. It is also extremely beneficial for lower back pain from which over 75 million Americans are said to suffer. Patting this area facilitates the passage of *ch'i* through the channel of control. It is important to include the entire area of the lower back, including the dorsal portions of the waist. In the Song of the Thirteen Movements from the *T'ai Chi Ch'uan Classic*, it says, "When the *Wei Lu* (lower part of the spinal cord) is centralized and erect, then the spirit of vitality raises up to the top of the head." During meditation, concentration on this area will produce heat, which also aids hormone production and glandular function.

157

CHIA CHI

The fourth psychic center is called *Chia Chi*, Middle Spine. It refers to the portion of the back at the lower edge of the rib cage and includes the acupuncture points *Chi Chung* (lower), *Chung Shu* (middle) and *Chin Shu* (upper). (See points 6, 7 and 8 of illustration, page 96.) It is the midpoint of the Channel of Control and is related to the function of the stomach, small intestine, and pancreas. This area is the axis of the body and all hand movement originates here. Backaches in this area are often caused by lifting heavy objects by bending the back rather than the knees. The first aim of stimulating *Chia Chi* is to allow the *ch'i* to pass more freely. This is especially important for meditation and also makes the body movements more limber. Benefits to health include aiding digestion; strengthening liver function, including both purification and production of blood; and the prevention and cure of backache. Pat this area, with one hand at a time, as it is difficult to use both, using the thumb side of the fist.

T'AO TAO

The fifth psychic center is called *T'ao Tao* in Taoist meditation practice. It is located between the first thoracic and seventh cervical vertebrae, *Ta Chui*, or "Biggest Vertebrae." It is connected with the shoulders in a similar manner as the lower spine is connected with the hips. It is therefore subject to the same stagnation of energy caused by the interaction of a multitude of bones, ligaments, and muscles. Many people experience pain in this part of the body due to rheumatism, strain of vigorous arm movements, or the accumulated tension of modern living.

We pat this area to relax the muscles and ligaments, creating harmony in the joints and allowing the *ch'i* to flow freely. Use the open palm or the palm side of a loosely clenched fist.

First pat *Ta Chui* and then extend the area of patting both left and right to include the shoulders and the neck. This will prevent or cure shoulder tension and pain, stiff neck, and insomnia. It is also effective in reducing fevers.

YU-CHEN

The **sixth psychic center** is called *Yu-Chen*, Jade Pillow, and is the place where the head touches the pillow. After *Wei Lu* it is the most difficult place for the *ch'i* to penetrate as there are no muscles here, only bone and skin. This center relates to the medulla oblongata, which contains the respiratory and cardiovascular centers of the autonomic nervous system. It is a very important part of the body and injury to it can cause loss of consciousness. Therefore, we pat *Yu-Chen* very gently with the palm or palm side of the fist. Patting this area stimulates the brain and allows the *ch'i* to pass easily. It also helps avoid or cure headaches.

NI WAN

The seventh psychic center is called *Ni Wan*, located on the top of the head. Many arteries, veins, and nerves meet here, hence the name *Pei Hui*, meaning a Hundred Meetings in Chinese acupuncture. The brain is nearby as well as the spirit. The Taoists call this place *Shen Shih*, the Room of the Spirit, and consider this area to be its dwelling place. According to Taoist belief, when the highest levels of meditation are attained, the spirit may leave and enter the body at this point. Some schools of meditation locate this point just in front of a newborn's soft spot. Lao Tzu calls this the Gates of Heaven. In the *Tao Te Ching*, he says, "The Gates of Heaven Open and Close. Can you be like the Female?" He means, can you allow the spirit baby to pass through the Gates of Heaven as a woman gives birth to a child?

Ni Wan is also the highest point on the body. After the *ch'i* reaches here it becomes saliva and goes down to the mouth and throat. This saliva is sweet and nutritious. Therefore, Taoists call it "divine water." This process is similar to the distillation of water, in which water is heated to form vapor. This vapor rises up through tubing where it is cooled, then changed back into a liquid which drips down in a purified state. Since this part of the body consists of skin covering bone it is often difficult for the *ch'i* to pass through. We use psychic patting on the whole area of the top of the head to create harmony among the nerves, arteries, and veins and to allow the *ch'i* to pass freely. Use the palm side of a loosely closed fist to pat the whole area very lightly and gently forty-eight times. For health, patting this center is used to prevent and cure headaches and to prevent fainting.

TZU CH'IAO

The eighth psychic center is called *Tzu Ch'iao*, Cavity of the Ancestors. It is located in the middle of the head, behind the point between the eyebrows. This point is a place of concentration in Taoist meditation. According to Lu K'wan Yu,[1] concentration on this point can produce the spirit. When mature enough one can see the Golden Light. This light descends and combines with the *ch'i* (inner energy or vitality) in the *Tan T'ien* to form the elixir which will descend to the lower cavity. Then the circulation of the Water Wheel begins again (ascending through the *Tu Mo*, descending through the *Jen Mo*, and ascending again in the ceaseless motion of the wheel. Because of its role in forming the elixir, *Tzu Ch'iao* is also called the upper *Tan T'ien*, or upper elixir field. In Western anatomy this place corresponds to the pituitary gland which produces many important hormones regulating various physiological functions. This area is very important for health as both wisdom and insanity begin here. We pat this point with

[1]Lu K'wan Yu, *Taoist Yoga* (New York: Samuel Weiser, 1970) pp. 1-8.

a loosely closed fist or with the palm. In addition to *Tzu Ch'iao*, pat *Mien T'ang*, the Bright Hall, located about a half an inch above *Tzu Ch'iao*, and *T'ien T'ing*, the Court of Heaven, which extends from about two inches above *Tzu Ch'iao* to the hairline. Extend the patting to the left and right temples, very important areas for both the spirit and sensations. Patting this area allows the *ch'i* to pass freely, clears the mind, and is helpful in preventing headaches and eye problems.

CHUNG KUNG

The ninth psychic center is called *Chung Kung*, the Central Palace. It is located in the middle of the chest, below the level of the breasts and above the solar plexus. In Taoist meditation this center represents the heart and is called *Li*, which means fire, or the middle *Tan T'ien*. The lower *Tan T'ien* is called *K'an*, or water, and represents the kidneys. When the *ch'i* of the middle *Tan T'ien* joins with that of the lower *Tan T'ien* it is called the Lesser Heavenly Current, or the Union of *K'an* and *Li*, water and fire.

This center is closely connected with the function of the heart, lungs, liver, and thymus gland. In ancient times it was believed that the mind occupied the heart, making this center doubly important. However, medical doctors later discovered that this isn't so. Still, many important functions are related to this center including blood circulation, respiration, purification, and the immune system. Patting this area gently with the palm increases the production of heat and energy. It stimulates heart function thereby protecting the body from heart attack. It assists the function of the lungs and protects the body from tuberculosis and other respiratory problems. Liver function is enhanced, keeping the blood pure and the body protected from poisons and other toxic materials. It also strengthens the thymus gland which performs an important role in the body's immune system and may have a key role in the aging process. It is called "the mysterious thymus gland" since it seems to reach its fullest development at age fourteen, thereafter declining in size and function. By age fifty, it is reported, only 15 percent of the thymus gland remains. Stimulating the thymus gland by patting *Chung Kung* should help prevent the decline which accompanies aging.

TAI MO

The *Tai Mo*, or Belt Channel, is the tenth psychic center. We pat the entire channel as its most important function is to connect the *Jen Mo* and the *Ch'ueng Mo* (Thrusting Channel) and the back and front of the body. It begins just below the navel and extends left and right around the body curving upwards and ending in the area of the kidneys. (See page 98.) It may be more convenient to pat this area immediately after patting *Tan T'ien* and then continue to pat *Wei Lu*. Or, if *Tai Mo* is patted tenth, then continue upwards along the sympathetic nerve line (on either side of the spinal column) to the *Yang (Yu) Wei Mo*.

YANG (YU) WEI MO

Yang (Yu) Wei Mo, the Outside Arm Channel, is the eleventh psychic center and again includes the entire channel. It starts at the shoulders and runs down the outside of the arms to the fingertips. It continues up the inside of the fingers and ends in the middle of the palm where it joins with the *Yin (Yu) Wei Mo*. (See page 99.) Many people experience rheumatism or other types of pain in the shoulders and arms. Patting *Yang (Yu) Wei Mo* increases blood circulation and relaxes the bones, joints, and ligaments of the shoulders, elbows, and wrists. It is very beneficial for daily life as many activities depend on the arms. In China this channel could be patted for health or for relaxation. Chia Mu, a rich and noble old lady from the famous novel from the Ching Dynasty, *The Dream of the Red Chamber*, often had her maid servants pat this channel and her back for her. They used hammers made of soft wood or dried papaya attached to a flexible handle. If patting by yourself, use the left palm to pat the right side and the right palm for the left side, or have someone pat this channel for you.

YIN (YU) WEI MO

The *Yin (Yu) Wei Mo*, the Inside Arm Channel, is the twelfth psychic center. It begins at the middle of the palm, runs up the inside of the arm and ends in the upper torso, a few inches below the collarbone. (See page 99.) Pat this channel with the palms through its whole length and then pat down the front of the chest along the mammillary (nipple) line.

YANG CHIAO (MO)

The *Yang Chiao (Mo)*, the Outer Leg Channel, is the thirteenth psychic center. While it runs the whole length of the body, we pat *Yang Chiao* only in the legs. (See page 100.) The biggest arteries and veins, after those of the heart, are located in the legs, and are like two roots of a tree supporting the body. People who stand or sit a lot may experience stagnation of blood in the legs, and those who perform strenuous work often suffer stiffness. Patting can help both these conditions as well as paralysis, rheumatism, and other leg aches. We can pat *Yang Chiao (Mo)* ourselves while standing, sitting, or lying down, or have someone pat it for us. Use loosely clenched fists, starting at the side of the hips going down the outside of the legs to the ankles. Continue along the top of the feet, over the toes to the point in the middle of the bottom of the foot, one-third of the way from the toes to the heel, called *Yung Ch'uan*. This is where *Yang Chiao (Mo)* connects with *Yin Chiao (Mo)*.

Patting the legs increases the blood circulation and softens the blood vessels. It relaxes the muscles and joints and makes the ligaments more resilient. If we pat the legs daily we can avoid many leg problems, especially stiffness in the legs which often accompanies old age, for if the legs become too stiff, blood cannot nourish them at all and paralysis may result. However, consistent patting of the legs keeps them healthy by aiding blood circulation and cures the pains which so often make sleep difficult for older people. An example of this kind of patting is found in *The Dream of the Red Chamber*. After Chia Mu, the old lady mentioned above, leaves her daughter-in-law, she has the maid servants lower the bamboo curtain. They pat her legs and she falls asleep.

YIN CHIAO (MO)

The *Yin Chiao (Mo)* is the Inner Leg Channel and fourteenth psychic center. It starts at *Yung Ch'uan* on the bottom of the foot and goes up the inside of the leg to the pubic region. (See page 101.) While it continues up to the head, we pat it only in the legs. Patting *Yin Chiao (Mo)* strengthens the legs much as *Yang Chiao (Mo)* by increasing blood circulation and relaxing the muscles, joints, and ligaments. It also increases sexual energy.

YUNG CH'UAN

The fifteenth psychic center is *Yung Ch'uan* (Bubbling Spring), located one-third of the way from the toes to the heel in the center of the bottom of each foot. As mentioned earlier, this is the meeting place of *Yang Chiao (Mo)* and *Yin Chiao (Mo)*.

While this point is the psychic center, in patting we include the whole foot. The feet are the very lowest part of the body and in China are compared to the earth. They support the full weight of the body and are extremely important for walking and standing. They are also very complicated structures, composed of many small bones and ligaments. While there are few muscles in the feet, there is, down to the smallest toe, a complex system of arteries, veins, and nerve endings.

Even though the feet are the lowest part of the body, they are still connected to the head and all the inner organs through the system of meridian lines, which all either begin or end in the feet. Thus the feet are both a support for weight and an important conduit for energy channels. Maintaining the health of the feet is vital because if the legs or feet are injured, it not only affects the local area but can cause a serious disease in another part of the body.

Patting the feet can be done sitting on the floor or in a chair, by bending one leg and resting it on the other (see page 35). Use the palm to pat the bottom of the foot, or use the palm side of loosely closed fists to pat the top and bottom simultaneously. Pat forty-eight or more times on each foot. This will not only aid the health of the feet, but the whole body as well.

P'ENG TZU

Very little is known about the life of P'eng Tzu. The *Book of History* records that he was the grandson of Chuang Yu and the third son of Lu Chuang. His original name was Chien Kieng. The name P'eng Tzu came from the territory over which he ruled, the territory of P'eng. The Emperor Yao had given P'eng Tzu this territory as a fief. P'eng Tzu lived from the time of the Yao dynasty (2357-2283 B.C.) until sometime in the Shang Yin dynasty (1783-1054 B.C.). When he was 767 years old, P'eng Tzu was still young and vigorous. News of this remarkable man reached the emperor of the Shang dynasty. The emperor sent for P'eng Tzu and asked him to reveal the secrets of health and exercise. P'eng Tzu agreed to teach him. The emperor found the method very effective. In order to preserve the secret, the emperor plotted to kill P'eng Tzu. Fortunately, P'eng Tzu learned of the plot and escaped. About seventy years later, he was seen in the Far Western territory.

P'eng Tzu's fief was my birthplace, now called Hsü Chou, in Kiang Su province, China. Its original name was P'eng Ch'eng. Many places in this region are named for P'eng Tzu: the great P'eng mountains (Ta P'eng Shan), the village of P'eng (P'eng Tzuin). P'eng's descendants in this region are many and prosperous.